The Awakening Giant

Above Loading coal, from Mayhew's *London Labour and the London Poor*, 1852

Overleaf The urban sprawl of nineteenth-century Birmingham

The
Awakening
Giant

Britain in the Industrial Revolution

E. R. Chamberlin

B. T. BATSFORD Ltd,
London & Sydney

ISBN 0 7134 3053 2

Filmset by Servis Filmsetting Ltd, Manchester
Printed by The Anchor Press, Tiptree, Essex
for the Publishers B. T. Batsford Ltd,
4 Fitzhardinge Street London W1H 0AH
23 Cross Street Brookvale N.S.W. 2100 Australia

Acknowledgment

The Author and Publishers would like to thank the following for their
kind permission to reproduce copyright illustrations: the Mansell Collection for pages 1, 2–3, 3, 4, 5, 25, 26, 27, 30, 40, 47, 48, 53, 56, 66, 67, 69,
75, 79, 80, 81, 83, 86, 87, 92, 93, 107, 109, 126, 128, 134, 142, 143, 145,
150, 154 (*top*), 156, 159, 162; Mary Evans Picture Library for pages 59,
71, 85, 108, 111, 123 (*left*), 130, 136, 140, 146–7, 149, 157; the National
Portrait Gallery for pages 131, 158; Glasgow Art Gallery and Museum
for pages 6–7; the Radio Times Hulton Picture Library for pages 11,
15, 16, 17, 20, 21, 28–9, 45, 51, 62–3, 65, 88–9, 96, 99 (*right*), 105, 113
(*right*), 114, 115, 118, 120, 121, 124, 132, 133, 139, 152, 165; the Victoria
and Albert Museum for pages 58, 161, 163; the Greater London Council
for page 99 (*left*); the Science Museum, London, for pages 10–11, 12–13, 19,
31, 32, 33, 36–7, 73, 76, 82; *Punch* for page 154 (*bottom*); the Royal Academy
of Arts, London, for page 78; the Post Office for page 22; the University
of Reading, Museum of English Rural Life, for pages 38–9, 44; National
Monuments Record for page 50; and Jonathan M. Gibson for pages 50–1
(*centre picture*).

Above Workers in an iron foundry, 1802

Opposite A Jewish pedlar, 1807

Contents

Introduction:
The Industrial Revolution

In 1811 Henry Bell's steamship *Comet* took the waters of the Clyde; John Knox's oil painting commemorating the event, shown on pages 6–7, can be seen as an allegory of what was about to happen to Britain, and to the world.

In the foreground of the picture two people are resting in an idyllic landscape that is bathed in the rich light of early evening. Cattle are grazing near them and in the middle distance are well spaced, well proportioned houses each with its park of generous trees. The Clyde cuts across the centre of the picture – a full-bodied, clean, blue-grey river under a fresh blue sky. The river is dotted all over with the towering white sails of ships: they are working ships but they fit comfortably into that natural background for their hulls are of timber and their motive power elemental. But in the centre of the picture, a dark smudge of smoke is forming over one of these vessels – Bell's *Comet*. At this point in time the smudge is insignificant, like a dirt mark made by a finger, but rapidly it will grow and grow, enveloping and changing the rich and peaceful scene.

The term 'Industrial Revolution' is very much a shorthand term invented for the convenience of historians. It is almost infinitely adjustable, capable of being contracted virtually to nothing, or expanded to take in centuries. Notoriously, a term which implies anything as abrupt as a revolution is completely inappropriate to describe a process which was produced by the slow movement of centuries. Watt's perfection of the steam engine came 2,000 years after Hero of Alexandria had demonstrated his elegant little steam toys; a large part of the textile industry of Nottingham was using, in the nineteenth century, machines which had been invented nearly four centuries earlier; the enclosures of the eighteenth century which altered the very pattern of the land were the final, accelerated stage of a process which had begun in Elizabethan England when the lamentation was heard that 'sheep were eating up men'.

An historian of the year 2,500, looking back with lordly detachment on the social and technological upheavals of our day, would probably consider himself perfectly justified in defining, as the Industrial Revolution, the period extending from approximately the 1720s to the 1970s. It possesses a homogeneity at least as great as that possessed by the Hundred Years' War, the Renaissance, the Dark Ages or any of the other labels we have pasted over arbitrary slices of time. There is a logical progression from the first wheezing steam locomotive to Sputnik 1; the hovercraft is a far closer relative to Brunel's *Great Britain* than this first steamship was to the sailing craft of its own day; the switch from organic to mineral fuel was a greater break with the past than the change from mineral to nuclear fuel.

In seeking to define the classical Industrial Revolution the historian is hampered by the fact that it spans two dynasties. The habit among monarchies of dating their past in terms of dynastic succession does at least give their history a sense of continuity. But when one dynasty succeeds another in an age of social change the effect can be profoundly misleading. Superficially, the Georgian and Victorian periods appear the complete antithesis of each other. The one conjures up a vision of mellowness, of aristocrats and peasantry pursuing immemorial occupations in a serene sunset – a classical landscape with figures as in Knox's painting. The other is a picture out of hell – an urban landscape peopled with gaunt and haunted figures, sulphurous with industrial smoke. Yet Abraham Darby was experimenting with iron production as early as 1709, and Coke of Norfolk was pottering around Holkham into the 1840s.

The student of the Industrial Revolution is further hampered by the fact that no great historian has arisen to put his impress upon the concept as Gibbon did for the end of the Roman Empire, as Burckhardt for the Renaissance, or even Clarendon for the Rebellion. Historical figures survive on a completely accidental basis. James Watt has entered legend with his boiling kettle – but Thomas Savery is scarcely more than a name and a title. 'In the gallery of inventors some canvases are too large, some should not be there at all and many deserving ones have not yet been painted, much less hung.'

Nevertheless, while it is easy to marshal a host of arguments to prove that the Industrial Revolution is a figment of the academic imagination, stubbornly it exists in its own right for it possesses characteristics which, in combination, make it unique. There is the enormously expanding population, which leaped from $6\frac{1}{2}$ million in 1750 to 9 million in 1800, and thence to 14 million in 1831. Concomitantly, there is the massive shift of population from country to town: in 1790 the country had twice as many inhabitants as the towns; in 1840 the proportion was almost exactly reversed. At the same time, there was an immense increase in the supply of food. In the north, the handsome town halls begin to appear as evidence of wealth and power. The face of the countryside begins to change, not only through enclosures but through the appearance of the straight lines of canals and railways – the first such lines since the days of the Romans. The recording of time becomes a major preoccupation. There is the continuous stimulus of war.

A man born in 1760, when George III ascended the throne, would have known 30 years of warfare – if only as a taxpayer – by the time he was 54 and read the news that Napoleon was in exile.

But the dominant characteristic, above all, was the staggering increase in the sheer number of 'things', of articles manufactured by the machine, that suddenly appeared on the planet. The editors of the massive *Oxford Dictionary of Technology* note ruefully that their Volume I comfortably covered all history from the beginning of time down to the year 500 BC. Volume II took the next millennium in its stride, but Volume III covered only 250 years, while it required all of Volume IV to record the technological achievement of the hundred years from 1750. It is those hundred years which form the span of this book.

A Whitsuntide excursion, 1783

The changing face of nineteenth-century Britain: Stephenson's Britannia tubular bridge being built over the Menai Straits, 1849

Festive spirit at the opening of the
Stockton–Darlington Railway, 27 September 1825

1 The Conquest of Space

Roads

Nearly 2,000 years after Rome had bound the nations of the West into a political whole, using her incredible road system as a ligature, the inhabitants of the British Isles were struggling to communicate with each other down tracks that might have been created by savages. In 1770 that indefatigable traveller Arthur Young raised his voice to curse those responsible for the road that ran south from Newcastle: 'A more dreadful road cannot be imagined. I was obliged to hire two men at one place to support my chaise from overturning. Let me persuade all travellers to avoid this terrible country, which must either dislocate their bones with broken pavements, or bury them in sand.'

But there was, it seemed, a still more dreadful road. A little later he was struggling to find epithets to describe the roads of Essex, the worst 'of all the cursed roads that ever disgraced this kingdom'. In some parts of the country men had turned their backs upon the wheel as being too sophisticated a device for prevailing conditions, and had resorted again to the prehistoric sledge. It was heavy and clumsy, but it could at least be dragged bodily through the morass that went by the name of road. Over perhaps half of the year, the wise traveller on horseback would ride parallel to the highway, on the comparatively firm turf of meadowland or even the earth of ploughland, rather than oblige his wretched mount to slosh its way through the mud of the so-called highway. Enclosure made this way of escape increasingly difficult, for the enclosed lands were now jealously hidden behind quick-growing hedges. On the worse stretches of the roads, therefore, a kind of causeway of large stones was laid along which packhorses, and the mounts of the gentry, could pick their way.

Separate from the highways were the great drove roads – a heritage from the dim, undocumented past. The ancestors of these drove roads were the tracks of Neolithic nomads, broadened and adapted at last for the passage of great herds of cattle between village and market town. Along most of its length the course of the drove road was clear enough, but where it crossed a moor or common the drover navigated much as a sailor might, taking his bearings from familiar landmarks.

Movement along the drove roads was periodic: weekly or monthly to market, or seasonally as cattle were moved from one area to another to be fattened. Nobody planned the movements; they took place as instinctively as the migration of the birds, obeying a scarcely understood economic law. Around the major cities of the country – in particular around

Cattle following a drove road

London – heavy traffic swamped the available tracks and cattle forsook the drove roads to take to the highways. The effect upon the already abysmally bad highways continued well into the era of macadamized roads: in the 1820s extra horses had to be harnessed to all stagecoaches approaching or leaving London, to help them over the terrible roads.

The most common traveller on the highways was the packman, who carried his wares from village to village, acting unconsciously as a vital medium of communication. Sometimes he was a simple pedlar; occasionally he rode proudly at the head of a string of 20 or more heavily laden animals, bound perhaps for one of the great fairs. Few villages, as yet, had their shops. Even in the opening decades of the nineteenth century, the irascible writer William Cobbett inveighed against shops as dastardly novelties designed to relieve honest men of their hard-earned cash. The alternative to patronizing the packman was to make a long, tiring and sometimes dangerous journey to the nearest market town. Few men enjoyed such a journey and so the packman who brought news, necessities and luxuries from the outside world was always sure of a welcome. He had disappeared almost completely by the 1850s, when W. B. Donne wrote his nostalgic description which contrasted the packman with the depressed pedlar or the licensed hawker

A packman on his lonely journey: crossing the ancient causeway in Cock Mill Wood

who followed in his steps:

> He was as loquacious as the barber . . . as ubiquitous as the wandering Jew. He had his winter circuit and his summer circuit: he was as regular in the delivery of news as the postman: nay, he often forestalled that government official in bringing down the latest intelligence of a landing on the French coast: of an execution at Tyburn: of prices in the London markets. He wrote love letters for the village beauties: he instructed alehouse politicians in the last speech of Bolingbroke, Walpole or Pitt. His tea, which often had paid no duty, emitted a savour and fragrance unknown to the dried sloe leaves vended by ordinary grocers. He was the purveyor for village songsters, having ever in his pack the most modern and captivating lace and ribbons, and the newest song and madrigal. He was competent to advise in the adjustment of knots and farthingales, and to show rustic beaux the last cock of the hat and the most approved method of wielding a cane.

The packman had come down from the remote past, lineal descendant of the Phoenician trader with his packs and his wiles and his resilience. And now he himself was moving into history, banished by the village shop which was, in its turn, brought into existence by safer roads.

By the mid-eighteenth century three quite distinct factors coincided to produce a vastly improved road system in all the advanced countries of Europe. These three factors were the revival of scientific interest in road-building that was itself a product of the revival of learning, the technical need for a good surface as a result of the widespread use of coaches and, above all, a central government prepared to recognize the necessity of good road communications and to do something about it. In England the first result was, characteristically, a compromise – the turnpike trusts. These were empowered by Parliament but ran their own affairs autonomously. The first was established on the Great North Road in 1663 and consisted simply of a bar laid across the road. When the system was revived in the eighteenth century, it introduced the gate and toll-house which figure so large in the literature of the period.

Between 1760 and 1800 Parliament established over 1,000 of these trusts. Each was responsible for the upkeep of a particular stretch of road, and was entitled to levy tolls for the purpose. Charges were high – by the 1820s the driver of a four-horse carriage had to pay at least 2s (10p) to traverse the road of any given trust, and he might have to pass through half-a-dozen or more turnpikes during the course of his journey. But less than 20 per cent of the total mileage of roads in Britain were under turnpike trust maintenance, and between the segments

were long stretches of road known as 'township roads'. These were maintained by parishes and, in the words of the novelist Robert Surtees, 'repaired in the usual style with mud and soft field stones that turned up like flitches of bacon'.

Dodging the turnpike tolls soon became a national sport. Some people even went to the trouble of training dogs to pull their carriages, thus avoiding the tax on 'carriages drawn by horses or beast of draught'. Even when he had paid his toll, the would-be traveller was subject to the most stringent regulations – mostly relating to the width of carriage wheels. Narrow wheels, shod as they were with iron, simply cut the road to ribbons. On some turnpikes, the coachman had to single up his horses, for they were forbidden to travel two abreast for fear of breaking up the causeway in the centre of the muddier roads.

Administratively inefficient though they were – perhaps half of the toll money collected actually went to road maintenance – the turnpikes were an immense advance on the previous system of parish levies. And when, in the closing decades of the eighteenth century, the deceptively simple innovations of Thomas Telford and John Loudon Macadam were adopted by the trusts Britain almost overnight had a road system that was

17

safe, fast and comfortable – although still operating over definitely limited areas.

Thomas Telford was one of the extraordinary Renaissance-type men whom the age was throwing up in prodigal numbers. His origins could not have been more humble. Born in a remote Dumfriesshire hamlet in 1757, his father was a shepherd and he himself herded cattle as a boy. At the age of 15 he was apprenticed to a mason; at 22 he was a journeyman earning 1s 6d ($7\frac{1}{2}$p) a day, and writing poetry in his spare time. It was good poetry – good enough to be published and good enough to be praised by no less a person that Robert Southey. But he kept his feet firmly on the ground: it was as engineer, not as poet, that 'Laughing Tam' envisaged his future. In 1780 he went to Edinburgh, at that time expanding with fantastic speed. Masons were in great demand there – but they were in London also and, two years later, the 26-year-old master mason took the inevitable road south.

A man of Telford's genius would have, eventually, made his own way upward – particularly in this period of fermenting intellectual and physical activity. The fact that Sir William Pulteney became his patron merely accelerated the process. Telford began his work in England by refurbishing the Pulteney seat at Shrewsbury, a comparatively frivolous task for one of his talents – but useful, because it brought him into contact with the landed classes of Shropshire. He soon became surveyor of public works for the county and then, in 1793, engineer for the Ellesmere Canal – the greatest work of its kind in the United Kingdom. The two aqueducts designed for it by the ex-mason were described as being 'among the boldest efforts of human endeavour in modern times'. Thereafter, great works poured from him: a design for a new London Bridge, to be executed entirely in iron and with only one arch across the wide river; the giant Caledonian Canal; and, above all, the Menai Bridge. Here, grace and power combined in a unique manner that was to be the badge of the dawning age. The bridge, designed to carry the Holyhead Road across the Menai Straits, took six years to build. The piers were an unprecedented 550 feet apart. The links of the great chains which held up the deck weighed 23 tons apiece and the bridge as a whole discharged its function without need for repair until 1939.

But important and dramatic though Telford's constructions were, they were overshadowed in social and economic history by the simple bits of broken stone with which he gave a smooth, hard surface to his roads. His first roadworks were for the

Shropshire turnpike trusts but, appropriately, it was in Scotland that he undertook his major work. The country had seen no roads built since the Rebellion of 1745, and Telford himself described the remarkable degree of isolation still in being at the turn of the century: 'The interior of the County of Sutherland was inaccessible: the only track lay along the shore among rocks and sands, which were covered by the sea in high tide.' Over some 18 years he built nearly 1,000 miles of road for his homeland, employing in all some 3,200 men and spending nearly a quarter of a million pounds. 'These undertakings may be regarded in the light of a working academy from which 800 men annually have gone forth improved workmen', he observed with justified pride.

Telford's revolutionary technique in roadmaking was simple enough. He built the foundations of his road solidly, as an honest stonemason should. But over the foundations he spread a layer of broken stones, each section small enough to pass through a two-inch ring. The more wear such a road received, the stronger it became as the traffic itself compacted the stones tighter.

Such, at least, was the theory. In practice, the laying of the solid, heavy foundations proved too expensive for general use. But even while criticisms were being levelled at the Telford construction, another Scotsman – John Loudon Macadam – provided a solution which was to bring roadmaking into the era of modern technology.

Macadam's social background was quite different from Telford's. His father, a banker, had died when young Macadam was only 14. The boy had been sent to live with a wealthy uncle in America and had remained there for some 20 years. Returning home to Ayrshire he became a magistrate, at the same time throwing himself into the problem of roadmaking and, in 1819, publishing his *Practical Essay on the Scientific Repair of Roads*. In this he enunciated a curious proposition, which was to change the whole technique of road-making and extend communications into every part of Britain: 'It is the native soil which really supports the weight of traffic: while it is preserved, it will carry any weight without sinking.' In other words, the whole purpose of roadmaking was to provide the earth with a protection from rain and frost. There was no need to provide massive, expensive foundations. Stones similar to those used by Telford – though preferably half-an-inch smaller – could be used without any other kind of foundation. They should be applied in three separate stages, with an interim between each stage during which traffic would do the work of

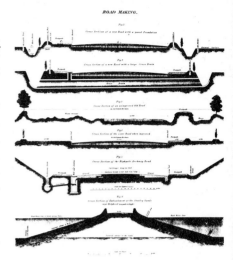

Cross-sections of different road surfaces, from Thomas Telford's *Road Making*, 1838

compacting the stones together.

As simple an invention as the wheel itself, macadamizing had almost as great an effect upon social history – shown by the speed with which it crossed first the English Channel and then the Atlantic. In America the first road to be macadamized was also the first national highway – the Cumberland Road, in 1832. Upon a macadamized surface the same horse could pull three times the load it had struggled with before and, for coaches, a lumbering average speed of about 3 mph shot up to 10 mph and even more on certain stretches. The new road system had an immediate effect not only upon volume and speed but also upon the type of traffic, and a bewildering variety of new wheeled vehicles appeared.

In the 1790s John Archer described the widely varying vehicles that transported a wealthy family between two of its estates as though it were taking part in a Roman triumph: 'First, the coach and six horses, with two postilions, coachman and three outriders. A postchaise and four posthorses: phaeton and four followed by two grooms, a chaise marine with four horses carrying the numerous service of plate – this last was escorted by the under butler, who had under his command three stout fellows: they formed part of the household and all were armed with blunderbusses.' Behind them were the traditional mounted servants: 'The hunters with their cloths of scarlet trimmed with silver and attended by the studgroom

Post chaise negotiating a steep descent: note the worn-out hacks and the strength needed to hold them up

and the huntsman: each horse had a fox's brush tied to the front of the bridle. The rear was brought up by the pack of hounds, the whipper-in, the hack-horses and the inferior stableman.'

A decade or so later a young swell like Lord Mutanhead, whom Mr Pickwick met in Bath, affected to ride in his own, personal mailcart: 'The neatest, pwettiest, gwacefullest thing that ever wan on wheels. Painted wed, with a cweam pie-bald . . . I dwove it over to Bwistol the other morning in a cwimson coat, with two servants widing a quarter of a mile behind. And confound me if the people didn't wush out of their cottages, and awest my pwogwess, to know if I wasn't the post. Glowious, glowious!'

By the early nineteenth century there were three major systems of travel. The wealthy man, naturally abhoring any public vehicle, went post – that is, he travelled in his own carriage, hiring horses at different stages en route. The less fastidious travelled by mailcoach and, from the 1820s onwards, by the fast efficient stagecoach.

In 1780 the postmaster's monopoly of carrying mails ended, enabling John Palmer to establish his mailcoach – a coach with an armed guard that carried both passengers and mail. The old system, although now collapsing, had at least established throughout the country the posting network which the coaches were to develop. The posthouses were inns and the landlord/postmaster had the double duty of maintaining the post-horse relays and delivering the mails within his area. Once, the postboy was the swiftest traveller on the road; now, on the

Mailcoach leaving Lombard Street at night

'Late for the Mail', 1848, from Fores's *Coaching Incidents*

smooth, hard surface of the new highways, the mailcoach could actually overtake him. But reliability was more important for the mailcoach than speed. It was the advent of the stagecoach that made speed a prime consideration, even greater than the passengers' comfort.

The coachmaster was essentially a man of the new age – an entrepreneur, a businessman controlling several hundred employees, making a hefty profit out of supplying a service but running the risk, too, of bankruptcy and ruination. His first necessity was a yard – usually, he simply obtained one of the larger inns and adapted it for its new role. It had to be large, for the coachmaster could be working anything up to 50 coaches. Naturally, only a few of them would be in the home yard at the same time, but they needed spare parts, maintenance, stabling and fodder. In addition there was the very modern, and ever growing, problem of paperwork: the booking in of passengers and the administrative work created by the very size of the organization.

The stagecoaches worked between recognized major centres of population: those based in London fanned out to such cities as Norwich, York, Shrewsbury and Bristol. The names they bore – the *Nimrod*, the *Wonder*, the *Times* – applied not to the individual coach but to the service. Over a 100-mile route there were usually at least two coaches, each bearing the same proud name.

The speed of the English stagecoaches became almost proverbial, a matter of envy for the Continentals. In 1803, it took three days to travel the 500 miles between Edinburgh and London. Just 15 years later the Norwich *Times* was covering the 112 miles to London in a single day. That speed was obtained not by flashy bursts of galloping but by maintaining a high average pace – between 8 and 10 mph – over the well-metalled roads and, above all, by the speed of changing horses at the stages. Gone was the old leisurely approach where the passengers had a chance to thaw out and have a hot meal and exchange social pleasantries. Now the coach-horse could be changed in under five minutes and the passengers bustled off again on the next stage of their journey, often still gulping and chewing. A new race of elite came into being – the coachmen of these crack vehicles. Even the young bloods of the town thought it an honour to share their high boxes and were prepared to back up their preference with golden guineas. Their less adventurous social equals paid for a seat inside. The rest clung, as best they could, on the swaying top, hedged round with parcels and baggage, well wrapped up against the ceaseless wind.

The heyday of the stagecoaches lasted scarcely 20 years, being finally ousted by the far faster railway. The coming of the railway, too, ended the turnpike system. It would have collapsed, in any case, of its own bad management: during the closing years it was estimated that some £85 were spent on every mile of turnpike against a revenue of £73. But the much abused system had again started the lifeblood of communication moving, if sluggishly, through the land.

Canals

The turnpikes and their ancillaries had an incalculable effect upon the circulation of ideas and fashions. But they were designed, essentially, for the movement of people. Animals still travelled along the drove roads and it was a long time before goods and raw materials were finally transferred from the sturdy backs of packhorses – each of which could carry three hundredweight or more – to enormous clumsy wagons drawn by teams of six or more horses. Early in the eighteenth century the novelist Daniel Defoe wrote of the hazards that awaited these wagoners. Describing the enormous trees carted from Sussex to Chatham for shipbuilding, he remarked: 'Sometimes I have seen one tree on a carriage, which they call there a tug, drawn by two and twenty oxen and even then it is carried so little a way, and then thrown down, and left for other tugs to take up and carry on, that sometimes it is two or three years before it gets to Chatham: for if once the rains come, it stirs no more that year.'

The system, such as it was, worked reasonably well for the unhurried world of the early eighteenth century. But with the development of industry and the consequent need for swift transportation of fuel and raw material in bulk, the pattern changed. A shipbuilder at Chatham, waiting for his tree, could comfort himself with the thought that it was being nicely seasoned during its long journey. But an ironmaster in Coalbrookdale, watching his precious stock of coal run down, was unlikely to adopt a similarly philosophic approach.

There was, in fact, already an ideal system for the cheap and relatively rapid movement of bulk commodities. Coal had been transported by sea for over two centuries, and by 1700 more than half Britain's shipping fleet was engaged in the humdrum task of carting coal southward down the coast from the mouth of the River Tyne. A ship could carry hundreds of tons, but each packhorse could bear the weight of only three hundred-weight of coal, and transportation overland more than a few miles from port or pithead made the use of coal prohibitively expensive. But, as ever, economic pressure created a technological solution: the rivers of Britain were ready-made water-roads, needing only channels – canals – to connect them.

One of the first attempts to render a river system navigable took place in Surrey. In 1635 Sir Richard Weston of Sutton Place obtained a commission from King Charles I to improve the navigation of the little River Wey. Weston had a strong personal interest in canals, for his low-lying lands at Sutton Place were continually flooded, and it was probably with the limited intention of flood control that he introduced the new-fangled Dutch device of pound locks upon the river. His later elaborate plan to make the river navigable to the Thames received a check during the Civil War (1642–49) but, despite his strong royalist sympathies, he was able to get an Act passed in 1651 which provided for the building of the Wey Navigation.

This early attempt was a failure – partly, perhaps, because there was as yet no economic need for a system of bulk transport, and partly because there were no great centres of population or industry in Surrey apart from London. Weston died and his son George was first obliged to sell the family shares in the business, and then actually found himself in prison, for the debts contracted by his father. The financial disputes dragged on for nearly 20 years before a second Act was obtained, in 1671, which put affairs in order. On the new basis the Wey Navigation entered a period of modest success, establishing a countryside network during the following century. By 1776 some 16,000 tons of merchandise were passing annually down to London, bringing renewed prosperity to the trading towns on the banks of the Wey.

But it was in the north, among the coalmines and the suddenly burgeoning factories with their insatiable demands for fuel and raw materials, that the canal age took its distinctive form. The dynamism was provided by a bored, restless, highly intelligent young aristocrat – Francis Egerton, Duke of Bridgewater. He was not quite 24 years old when, tiring of London society and, it was said, heartsick of an unrequited love affair, he threw himself into a project that his father had begun. The Bridgewater income was largely derived from coalmines at Worsley, and profits would be enormously increased if the coal could be cheaply moved in bulk to the booming town of Manchester. Bridgewater sought an engineer to help him

Perspective, sections and plan of a canal, from an early nineteenth-century handbook

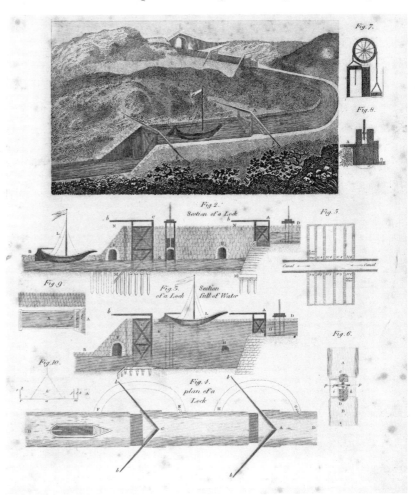

achieve this, and found him in the person of James Brindley.

Brindley's career was much like Telford's had been, much like so many other of the engineers who were reshaping the face of Britain. He was born of very poor parents, displayed a talent for handling machinery that amounted to genius and, in 1754, was taken into the Bridgewater service. The problem that the Duke laid before him was immense: the canal had to start underground at the coalworkings and, on its journey to Manchester, had to cross the River Irwell as well as a number of roads and smaller streams. To solve it, Brindley adopted the idea of the Roman aqueduct and built an immensely strong structure of stone, making the bottom of the duct watertight with thoroughly kneaded clay. The point where the canal crossed the River Irwell quickly became a great tourist attraction. Crowds came from all parts of the country to marvel at the spectacle of water crossing water and of ships travelling serenely high up in the air.

Brindley's canal was a great economic as well as an engineering feat, since coal could now be transported to Manchester at half the original cost. Soon the Duke of Bridgewater was planning an ambitious extension of the system – ambitious not only in the physical problems that had to be overcome but also

Water crossing water: the aqueduct over the River Irwell at Barton, the most famous of the canal aqueducts

Brindley's Bridgewater Canal, shown entering the underground coal workings at Worsley

in the complex financing that the work required. The Grand Trunk Canal, as the development was called, was begun in 1766 and took over 11 years to complete – 11 years in which capital was tied up and an army of men had to be moved from point to point. The Grand Trunk was Brindley's child – but he drove himself, as ever, unremittingly and died five years before the canal was completed at the age of 56. Brindley was a genuine original, a genius produced in response to the needs of his time. He was a rough diamond who never acquired social polish despite his fame and the fact that he rubbed shoulders with the 'quality'. He worked by a process of sheer dogged mental effort – habitually, when faced with an unusually knotty problem, he took to his bed, withdrawing wholly from society while that powerful, untrained brain ground out the required answer. He was single-minded to the point of fanaticism. A committee once asked him what was the use of rivers. 'To feed canals', was his characteristically laconic retort.

Brindley's first canal had cautiously followed the contours of the land, winding to and fro upon itself in order to achieve the vital necessity of a level surface. When he came to design the Grand Trunk Canal, he was more confident of his ability and more daring in his plans. This canal was to travel in a much straighter line: 76 locks were built along its 93-mile length and the canal was carried through five tunnels. One of these – the famous Harecastle Tunnel – extended for 2,880

yards. Brindley showed that canals could be constructed economically and operated effectively, and other engineers rapidly followed his lead. One of the engineers working on the Grand Trunk Canal was the young Thomas Telford, and when he turned to canal building on his own, his approach was Roman in its directness. Not for him the sinuous, if attractive, winding route to skirt natural obstacles – his canals were to go through, or above. Over the River Dee he threw an aqueduct 1,000 feet long, towering more than 120 feet in the air, herald of the enormous structures that the railway age would soon demand. The great spine of the Pennines was a challenge, not a barrier, to these immensely confident men. The Huddersfield Canal passed through the Standedge Tunnel at a height of 637 feet above sea-level, and the tunnel itself was nearly 5,500 yards long, almost double that of the much vaunted Harecastle Tunnel.

By the 1820s there were over 3,000 miles of canals, creating their own subculture. In the early days, the more respectable trading towns on the routes of the canals feared the prospect of an invasion of rough, itinerant bargemen and some even managed to force the payment of a toll upon the canal companies. But by the second decade of the nineteenth century the bargemen were accepted and even, in places, welcomed. According to one observer, they actually seemed to be a different race from the townsmen – trim and sailorlike in their dress and self-respecting in their habits. Unlike so many of those caught up in the industrialization of Britain their way of life was hard but it was also healthy. The normal craft used for bulk carriage displaced some 20 tons and usually, but by no means always, it was drawn by a single horse. On many stretches of canal, however, the motive power was supplied by the bargeman himself. In the earlier period, the tunnels through which the canal passed had no towpaths and the bargeman was obliged to propel his craft by lying on his back and kicking against the roof. It was a gruelling task in the pitch-darkness of a tunnel that might extend for more than two miles and certainly it was no work for a man who suffered from claustrophobia. Wages at first were low, but as the canal owners felt the competition first of the stagecoach and then of the railway, bargemen's wages rose accordingly.

By contrast with the bargeman, the life of the lock-keeper was hard. The bargeman had to be prepared to load and unload his craft and, if necessary, pull it along himself. The lock-keeper had a bewildering variety of tasks. Collecting tolls, checking loading, patrolling his section of the canal, main-

The high aesthetic qualities of the canal: the Rolle Canal at Torrington, Devon

taining equipment, regulating the flow of water and repairing broken embankments – all this fell to his lot, as well as the necessity of always being on hand to operate the lock. On the credit side, he was furnished with a small house and could eke out low wages by growing vegetables in the little garden behind.

The heyday of the canals was during the first four decades of the nineteenth century. Scarcely had they achieved their peak efficiency when they were challenged by the newest of all forms of locomotion, the railway. A writer in a Sussex magazine pointed out the contrast between the two systems in a colourful but not inaccurate piece of reportage. He described how, on his journey in a boat, he was temporarily imprisoned in a lock on a canal that ran parallel to a railway:

The horse that draws our boat is quietly feeding on the banks of the canal. As we remain here, languidly waiting to be liberated from the lock, along comes 'Puffin' Billy' flying over the iron rails like a mad thing. 'Phew,' whistles the locomotive. 'Puff, puff, puff,' retorts the engine and as we look round, the whole train of carriages whisks out of sight, leaving the smoke from the tunnel to slowly settle itself. The contrast is funny. While we have been fudging about in the dock, the engine has possibly flown ten miles with its freight.

Then, with percipience, the writer concluded: 'Is there anyone among us who can read the future and tell us whether the great iron railways which now spread all over the land will not some day be grown over with grass, having succumbed to a superior form of locomotion?'

But at the time he was writing, the railway was the force of the future, overshadowing road and canal alike.

Railways

In 1860, just three years before he died, William Makepeace Thackeray looked back on his life and pinpointed a moment of profound and universal change: 'Your railroad starts the new era, and we of a certain age belong to the new time and the old one. We elderly people lived in that pre-railroad world, which has passed into limbo and vanished from under us. I tell you it was firm under our feet once, and not long ago. They have raised those railroad embankments up, and shut off that old world that was behind them. Climb up that bank on which the irons are laid and look to the other side – it is gone.' Thackeray's rhetoric gave colour, but did not exaggerate: the coming of the railway drew a thick line between a past that receded into the mists of prehistory, and a future that would take man off the planet itself. More than any other invention, steam locomotion broke with the past for it was totally without precedent and the effect of its development could in no way be predicted.

The development of the canals – even the development of macadamized roads – were the result of a deliberate act of creation. The development of the 'permanent way', the vital prerequisite to steam locomotion, took place over many years. Certainly no record was made of the unknown man who, in order to facilitate the passage of a heavily laden wagon over soft or rough ground, laid a track for the wheels. The technique was probably first introduced in the collieries. The need to transport large quantities of coal from one fixed point to another a short distance away – from the colliery to the loading dock of the nearest port – quite casually and inevitably produced a species of railway. The regular and frequent passage of the heavily laden wagons churned up the road, and it was commonsense to lay down baulks of wood. Sooner or later it became obvious that if wagons could be dispersed at collecting and discharge points, the work of loading and unloading would be greatly speeded. From this simple observation sprang the concept of the marshalling yard and that, in turn, gave birth to the idea of guiding the wheels of wagons in this direction by means of the railroad itself.

From the provision of baulks of wood as a firm footing to the

The ancestor of the railway: a horse-drawn coal wagon running on rails, 1764

invention of shaped metal rails was a wide but not unprecedented leap. James Brindley had made a similar jump when he
conceived the idea of the artificial waterway instead of the
modified natural river. In 1767, at Coalbrookdale in Derby,
Richard Reynolds constructed the first complete track of cast-
iron rails, furnished with flanges to guide the wheels. The
track was intended to be temporary, a means of utilizing the
iron during a period of slump. It was so astonishingly successful
that other collieries and ironworks quickly followed suit. In
1801 the first Railway Act was passed to allow the construction
of the Surrey Iron Railway between Wandsworth and Croy-
don. Four years later this was declared open – it was Britain's
first public railway.

Despite its grand title, the Surrey Iron Railway was intended
only to transport merchandise the short distance from Wandsworth to the outskirts of London. Its importance lay in the
publicity that attended its opening, when its efficiency was
dramatically demonstrated. Six wagons were loaded with
stone, each loaded wagon weighing some three tons, and were
linked together. A single horse was harnessed to the leading
wagon and moved the 18 tons deadweight, pulling it with ease
over the six-mile distance. During the journey other wagons
were added until, over the last stretch, the horse was pulling
55 tons at a little under 6 mph. Under normal conditions, a
horse on a good road can pull a laden wagon of about 15 cwt,

Toll sheet for the world's first railway.
The railway was used for transporting
bulk cargoes from Wandsworth to
Carshalton

and then only for a short distance.

Despite the impressive demonstration, no immediate attempt was made to develop the railroad system. The canals were then at the peak of their efficiency and there was not sufficient economic pressure to make it worthwhile investing in a new method. It was not until 1818, over 13 years after the Surrey experiment, that a group of Quaker businessmen decided to build a railroad between Stockton and Darlington in order to transport coal. The Bill was rejected three times before Parliament passed it at last in 1821 – an indication of the opposition that the development of railways was to meet over the next two decades. Having obtained parliamentary approval, the consortium turned to the technical problem of the motive power that was to be used on their railroad. Energetically, their engineer told them that there was truly only one means of locomotion to be considered and that was steam. The engineer's name was George Stephenson.

Stephenson was yet another man from the lowest level of society who found himself borne up to dizzy heights by the new technological spirit. The occurrence was so constant that it seemed almost as though a law were in the making – a law which stated that a virgin mind, unmoulded by accepted forms of education, could best grasp and control the titanic and wholly unprecedented powers now being unleashed. Like his father, Stephenson became a colliery fireman – and not until he was 18 years old did he learn to read and write. Later, he worked as a brakesman – the man who controls the winding engine of the colliery – and by dismantling and assembling the engine in his rare spare time he taught himself the elements of steam power.

Steam locomotion was a dominant speculative subject in the world of engineering at the turn of the eighteenth century. Since 1784, when James Watt's assistant William Murdoch had made a working model of a steam engine, successive experimental engineers had wrestled with the problem of designing a steam engine powerful enough to provide loco-motion but also small enough to be mobile.

A Cornish engineer, Richard Trevithick, successfully placed a steam carriage on the road in 1801. It was little more than a curiosity, but three years later he made the vital union between steam-power and railroad that was to change the face of civilization. In 1808 he brought his railway to London, setting it up as a kind of circus show in a circular enclosure. The crowds who flocked to buy tickets to ride behind the locomotive were doing so only for a passing amusement – but

My ride with Trevithick in the year 1808 in an open carriage propelled by the steam engine of which the enclosed is a print, took place, then a Waste here now Torrington Square.

TREVITHICKS,
PORTABLE STEAM ENGINE.

Catch me who can.

Mechanical Power Subduing Animal Speed.

Trevithick's steam engine 'Catch Me Who Can', 1808. The scribbled note on the left refers to the circular railway which Trevithick staged as a public entertainment (*see below*)

they were the world's first train passengers.

In considering the motive power best suited to the Stockton-Darlington line, young George Stephenson's mind inevitably turned towards steam locomotion. In 1813 he had developed a locomotive which could pull 30 tons up an incline, proving conclusively that there was no need to provide complex cogs and ratchets, but that a smooth wheel could run perfectly efficiently on a smooth rail. His enthusiasm for the new propulsive power, coupled with his manifest skill as an engineer, banished the last lingering doubts in the directors' minds regarding the virtue of steam over horse-power. On 27 September 1825, Stephenson's *Locomotion No 1* steamed out of Darlington hauling six wagons filled with coal and flour, a hastily converted coach for the directors, 21 coal wagons fitted up with seats for passengers and finally six more wagons filled with coal. A group of young men attempted to pace the roaring, smoking monster on horseback, but as the train steamed forward at a maximum speed of 15 mph it soon drew ahead of all riders.

Stephenson had proved that steam locomotion could work. Now he set out to prove that it could work regularly, predictably, reliably. Five years after *Locomotion No 1* had shown its paces, the *Rocket* hauled a trainload of distinguished guests from Liverpool to Manchester. The prospectus of the Liverpool and Manchester Company sounded the authentic accents of the new commercial age:

Trevithick's circular railway set up near Torrington Square: the combination of railway and steam engine, used here as a pastime, was to change the face of civilization

33

In the present state of trade and commercial enterprise, despatch is no less essential than economy. Merchandise is frequently brought across the Atlantic from New York to Liverpool in 21 days, while owing to various causes of delay goods have in some instances been longer in their passage from Liverpool to Manchester . . . Coal will be brought to market in greater quantity at reduced rates and farming produce of various kinds will find its way from greater distances at more reasonable rates.

The company amply justified its boast. The existence of the Stockton-Darlington Railway had cut the price of coal in Darlington from 18s to 8s 6d a ton, a staggering reduction which was the best possible advertisement for the Liverpool and Manchester Railway. By the second year of its operation, the saving in the carriage of cotton alone amounted to over £20,000 a year. But the phenomenal success of its passenger traffic was an even greater implication of social change. The directors had expected the transporting of passengers to earn the company about £10,000 a year; the actual sum earned was nearly ten times that amount. The company could well afford to be generous to the engineer whose combined qualities of vision and practical skill had made it possible. George Stephenson, the colliery fireman's son whose first paid employment was the herding of cows, now had a four-figure salary. It was the dazzling success of men like him, from the very lowest levels of society, that was to breed the sturdy Victorian belief summed up in the favourite phrase – 'God helps those who help themselves'. But it was also to breed the belief that the poor were poor because they wanted to be poor.

The Liverpool and Manchester Railway launched the railway boom – a wave of speculation that was almost as extreme, and as lunatic, as the South Sea bubble of the previous century. The greedy and the stupid were neatly matched by the criminal: some of the promoters finished up in prison but most made their fortune, the first of a new wave of self-made men. But certainly not all were enraptured by the awesome new transport system. The poet William Wordsworth wrung his hands:

> *Is there no nook of English ground secure*
> *From rash assault . . .?*
> *Plead for thy peace, thou beautiful romance*
> *Of Nature.*

The less fanciful Duke of Wellington deplored the railway, noting sourly that it 'would encourage the lower classes to

Picnicking by the side of the railway line: the terminus of the Garnkirk and Glasgow Railway c. 1845

move about' – an unusually perspicuous remark from His Grace. Dr Lardner proved conclusively that passengers would suffocate at the tremendous speeds. Innkeepers trooped forward to show how towns would die for want of trade as the railway swept potential customers onward at high speed. Canal trade would collapse, turnpikes come to an end and, as inevitable corollary, there would be less work for the poor who would become an additional burden on the rates. The nascent railway companies were forced to disburse hundreds of thousands of pounds in compensation for largely imaginary disadvantages: it was a comparatively simple task to blackmail them into paying vast sums for tiny, otherwise worthless strips of land that happened to lie across the advancing path of the railway. But despite the opposition, despite the enormous expenses, the railways spread like some vast natural force.

The very nature of the railroad – the necessity of establishing a solid, level surface across a widely varying terrain – created the biggest earthmoving operation in the history of humanity. 'Railway mounds, vaster than the walls of Babylon,' Ruskin intoned – and did not even begin to exaggerate. Peter Lecount, George Stephenson's principal assistant, accumulated some bizarre statistics to demonstrate the pharaonic scale of railway construction. In building the Great Pyramid, between 100,000 and 300,000 men had laboured for 20 years, lifting the equivalent of 15,733 million cubic feet of stone. In building the London-Birmingham Railway, less than 20,000 men, working for about five years, had raised 25,000 million cubic feet of material – over 9 million cubic feet more than had been shifted by King Cheops's men. The building of this railway alone was equivalent to building the Great Wall of China, Lecount claimed.

Charles Dickens, in *Dombey and Son,* described the building of this railway in terms that justified Lecount's boast. The engineers had to take the railroad through an immense cutting in Camden Hill and Dickens seems to have visited the site about half-way through the operation:

> The first shock of a great earthquake had rent the whole neighbourhood to its centre. Traces of its course were visible on every side. Houses were knocked down, streets broken through and stopped: deep pits and trenches dug in the ground: enormous heaps of earth and clay thrown up: buildings that were undermined and shaken, propped by great beams of wood. Here a chaos of carts, overthrown and jumbled together lay topsyturvy at the bottom of a steep unnatural hill: there, confused treasures of iron soaked and rusted in something that had accidentally become a pond . . . bridges that led nowhere: thoroughfares that were wholly impassable – Babel towers of chimneys . . . temporary wooden houses . . . carcases of ragged tenements, fragments of unfinished walls and arches . . . In short, the yet unfinished and unopened Railroad was in progress and, from the very core of all this dire disorder, tailed smoothly away, upon its mighty course of civilization and improvement.

Dickens's reaction – half horrified, half admiring – to the Camden Cutting was the reaction of Britain as a whole to its new acquisition.

The social effect of the railroad was immediate, widespread, cumulative: it seemed, indeed, that every aspect of it triggered off a chain reaction even in spheres not obviously connected to it. Thus the widespread availability of cheap coal not only made life slightly less unpleasant for the poor, but also led to the neglect of woodlands that had once provided the only fuel available. Decent women could, for the first time in history, travel unchaperoned – marginally contributing to female emancipation. For the town proletariat, stifling in the newly-made industrial slums, the countryside was brought a few pence and an hour or so away. For the village labourer, who had never travelled further than the nearest market town, the great metropolis was opened up, together with its unsettling ideas.

But the pessimists, too, were justified. The compact town, that had come down scarcely changed through the centuries, dissolved in the solvent of the railroad. Why live in the cramped

and stinking centre, when green fields could be had for the sake of a daily journey? The sprawl that was to be the blot on the face of late nineteenth-century England began. Similarly the social counterpart of the physical sprawl commenced. People moved away from the community where their forefathers had been born, married and died. The drift was slow, timid at first – a mile or so down the railroad – but then a little further, and a little further yet, beginning the process of fragmentation that was to be the great social scourge of the twentieth century. Class distinction, which had already begun with the collapse of the established society, now received specific and concrete form with the introduction of First, Second and Third Class travel. The resurrected roads grew quiet again – their quietest perhaps since the days of the Norman Conquest – and the great inns that stood alongside them decayed in consequence.

Inexorably the railway lines spread. In 1843 there were some 2,000 miles of track. Three years later only an additional 36 miles had been built. But within nine years – by mid-1855 – there were over 8,000 miles. Despite the plaints of the traditionalists and the gentry, the common people heartily approved of this common means of movement – as a writer in the *Illustrated London News* made very clear in December 1844:

Wonderful is the railroad transport of the present day. We are not of those who regret 'the good old coaching days' and 'the roadside inns'. Nor had that much coveted position, 'the box', any extraordinary charms for us. Beyond what was connected with the horses they were driving, and the public houses they passed, we generally found the coachmen mighty dull and heavy men. A few miles outside, in sunny weather, were all very well: but the cheerless umbrella-covered drag of a whole day – and night too – had in it nothing to regret. Who for one instant would compare the trouble and extortions of the old coachyard to the comfort of the station?

The confident present was deriding the benighted past – the writer spoke in the precise accents of his generation.

Navvies at work: excavating the Olive Mount Cutting on the Liverpool and Manchester Railway, four miles from Liverpool

Overleaf Thomas Coke inspecting some of his Southdown sheep, 1808. From the painting by Thomas Weaver

2 The Rural World

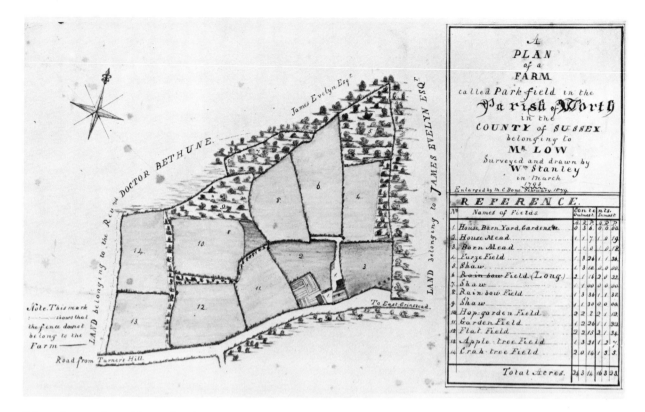

The Agrarian Revolution

The land through which the black fingers of the railroad were tentatively groping was going through a change as profound as that which affected the towns. It was a change that was, physically, immediately obvious – so much so that a man in his forties at the turn of the eighteenth century would scarcely recognize the village surroundings of his childhood. The ancient nucleus of manor, church and inn remained and would remain: it was the organic, living part of the village that had altered its appearance. Where the village had once stood at – or near – the centre of a huge, treeless, rather bleak field, it was surrounded now with neatly hedged smaller fields. Once, the villager could have walked for miles through the so-called waste or common land that surrounded the village holding. Now, he would be brought to an abrupt halt by a shoulder-high hedge of thorn, pretty enough in spring with its white or pink blossoms, but forming an impassable barrier nevertheless. From the hedges, and the coppices in between, rose hundreds of sturdy young trees – oak and elm for the most part – masking a landscape that once swept unbroken to the horizon.

Enclosure of lands had been going on for centuries, but on an *ad hoc* basis as the important landowners made private

Plan of enclosed fields: a Sussex farm in 1793

arrangements with their smaller neighbours. The pace began to accelerate in the early eighteenth century. There was no one obvious reason for the increase in pace except, perhaps, the self-evident fact that larger units of land were more efficiently farmed than small, isolated strips. From the 1750s Parliament took a hand in the process with the enactment of private Bills of Enclosure. The procedure was, in theory, admirably democratic: a given area could not be enclosed unless the owners of four-fifths of the individual strips assented. In fact, four-fifths of the strips could be owned by two or three wealthy farmers while the remaining one-fifth was split up among scores of men. But once the Bill had been passed, all holders of land in the village had no option but to be included in the scheme. They were not brutally dispossessed: again, in theory, a democratic inquiry was held by parliamentary commissioners whose task was to re-distribute the land and allocate either land or money, in compensation, to the smaller men. In practice, the commissioners were almost invariably drawn from the ranks of the major landowners, the very men who had promoted the Bill in the first instance and who now had a free hand to adjust the holdings so as best to suit their own convenience.

The pre-enclosure, openfield system had been the last vestige of the ancient system of land tenure which saw the use of soil as essentially the same as the use of air or water. The medieval feudal system had superimposed a social hierarchy upon that ancient fabric, yet even the most absolute feudal lord had hesitated to claim sovereignty over the common lands. The peasant farmer picked up his tiny strips of arable land in excactly the same way as the great man picked up his estates – by purchase or, more usually, by marriage and inheritance. But all had equal right to the common land. The nature of that land varied enormously according to the terrain. It could be meadowland or moorland, marsh, woodland, mountain or downland. The main use of the common land was, for the most part, for grazing, although that seems to have been poor enough under the best of circumstances: 'It is painful to observe the very wretched appearance of the animals who have no other dependence but upon the pasture of these commons, and who, in most instances, bear a greater resemblance to living skeletons than anything else,' the *Farmer's Magazine* noted as late as 1802.

Time has given the small strip farmers an aura of romance as the last survivors of a sturdy yeomanry. In fact, they seem to have combined to pull each other down to the lowest common level. Long after men like Jethro Tull and Lord

Combined drill plough and manure
spreader, invented in 1745. From *The
Farmer's Instructor*, 1747

This four Wheel Drill Plow with a Seed and a Manure Hopper, was first Invented in the Year 1745 and is now in Use with W.ᵐ Ellis at Little Gaddesden near Hempstead in Hertfordshire, where any person may View the same. It is so light that a Man may Draw it, but Generally drawn by a pony or little Horse—

Townshend had shown what could be done with systematic farming, the commoners continued with an agricultural system that merely exhausted the soil. It could hardly be otherwise, considering the physical nature of the holdings. Inconsistent in size and shape, dotted erratically over a wide area and, above all, subject to common rights of grazing between harvest and spring, their owners had limited control over them. Most were far too narrow to benefit from Tull's theory of cross-hoeing, and the man who experimented with a winter crop merely saw it devoured by his neighbour's cattle during the open winter season.

Nevertheless, the openfield system did give even the poorest man a stake in the land. This had a great psychological as well as a practical value. The small size of the strips meant that a poor but thrifty man could hope to add a few more to his holding during his life time. The common grazing land reared very poor cattle – but that was better than no cattle at all. The commoner could hope to maintain at least a cow, which would yield some milk for his children. The woodlands could support a few skinny pigs which, slaughtered in autumn, helped tide the family over the long, hungry winter. The common lands also provided wood, or at least dung, for fuel as well as a certain amount of timber and stone for building. In an era of subsistence farming, the meagre pickings provided by communal ownership could mean the difference between survival and starvation. Then, overnight, the commoner found himself dispossessed: some 4,000 Acts were passed between 1760 and 1820 during which five million acres of common land disappeared behind quickset hedges. The soaring food prices created by the Napoleonic Wars gave a powerful economic incentive to more rational farming. The strategic need encouraged Parliament to speed the process even further and a General Enclosure Act was passed, eliminating the tedious business of promoting individual Bills. The rights of the poor man were still, in theory, safeguarded. He did not necessarily lose his stake in the land: his share was rationalized, the scattered strips brought neatly together. All he had to do was pay the charges and put a fence round his new property. He was even given cash compensation for the lands he had lost to the larger landowners. But lawyers' fees were high; so too was the cost of fencing. Even when he went ahead and paid the fees and the cost of fencing, his small poor holding certainly could not support the cow and two or three pigs that were denied their ancient right of access to the common. There was little choice but to sell what little land he had and either hire himself out as a labourer or take the road that led to the industrial towns – the road which promised so much but which, for so many, was merely the path to a living hell.

Some of the dispossessed literally fell by the wayside. These were the ones for whom the cash payment proved a most fatal gift. Never before in their lives had they had so much gold in their pockets. The taverns welcomed them and, for a few weeks – or a few months – they knew the heady delight of dispensing largess, the numbing satisfaction of drinking hour after hour. 'Go to an alehouse kitchen on an old enclosed country [county] and there you will see the origin of poverty and the poor rates,' wrote Arthur Young. 'For whom are they to be sober? For whom are they to save – such are their questions. For the parish? If I am diligent, shall I have leave to build a cottage? If I am sober, shall I have land for a cow? If I am frugal, shall I have half an acre of potatoes? You offer no motives . . . Bring me another pot.' Then, at the end, nothing: sometimes not even a home, for their wretched cabin went with the land and the new master might not want such a worker.

This was the debit side – but even the censorius William Cobbett found himself admiring the technical results of enclosure. In one of his Rides, through Huntingdon, he noted that 'the fields on the left seem to have been enclosed by Act of Parliament and they certainly are the most beautiful fields that I ever saw . . . exceedingly well planted and raised'. Behind those rapidly growing thorn hedges, which separated the landless men from the man of property, there was occurring a revolution that was as profound and far-reaching as the revolution created by steampower. Indeed, in the extraordinary interlocking series of causes and effects that gave birth to a

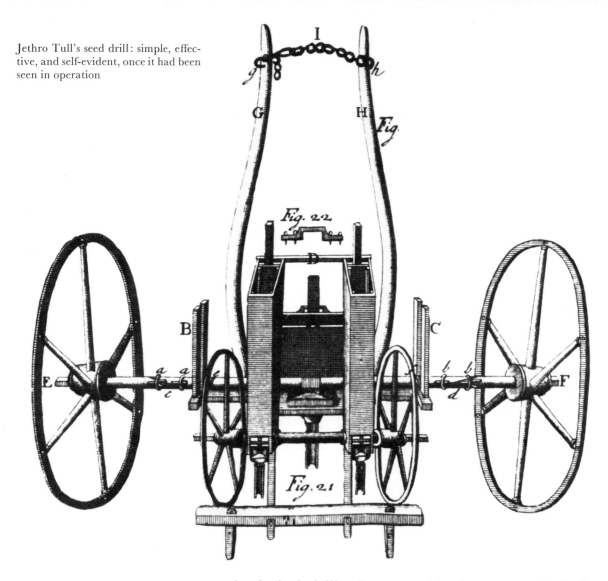

Jethro Tull's seed drill: simple, effective, and self-evident, once it had been seen in operation

technological civilization, arguably the greatest single factor upon which all else depended was this immense increase in the supply of food.

Some of the developments employed upon the enclosed lands were simple in themselves, or had actually been used abroad for decades. It was well over a century since Jethro Tull, the lawyer turned farmer, had demonstrated the incalculable value of deep-hoeing and of sowing seed in drills instead of scattering it broadcast. It was, perhaps, just as well that Tull's revolutionary theories took so long to be adopted – for they included a resolute refusal to pollute the soil with manure and a contemptuous rejection of the idea that, by rotating crops, yield could be maintained while the land was actually restored. But by the time Thomas Coke of Norfolk had launched his informal agricultural academy, the farming world was just sophisticated enough to reject Tull's more destructive theories while absorbing the positive.

In 1776, when the 22-year-old Thomas Coke inherited Holkham from his uncle, the estate was producing a revenue of £2,200. By 1816, this revenue had increased to £20,000 per annum, a tenfold yield that was due entirely to Coke. He was, in fact, ignorant of farming when he took over, and was faced almost immediately by a revolt of some of his larger tenants. They declined to renew their leases at the higher rents made necessary by soaring prices, probably gambling on the young man's inexperience. He promptly took over their lands himself, declaring that he would farm them personally.

It could have been a disastrous experiment, but the young man had the good sense to invite the local farmers to Holkham in order to gain the benefit of their deep, if rather narrow, farming experience. Imperceptibly, the student became the tutor and the organizer of a lively symposium. The occasion spontaneously developed around the annual sheep-shearing, when thousands of people attended from miles around. For the majority the Holkham sheep-shearing was simply a bigger and better fair than normally came their way. For a serious minority, it was an unrivalled opportunity to receive – and pass on – agricultural innovations. The usual procedure was for Coke to take his guests on a tour of the estate, which was followed about mid-afternoon by a lavish dinner. Up to 500

The dissemination of information: the Woburn sheep-shearing, 1811. The figure on horseback is the Duke of Bedford

guests were entertained and then, relaxed with good food and drink, they took part in a lively discussion in which the smallest tenant farmer could be as certain of a hearing as was the biggest landowner in the area.

The eclectic nature of Holkham was itself index to the character of Coke's agricultural experiments. He was not an originator in any true sense: rather he drew freely upon the ideas both of his contemporaries and of his predecessors, and was prepared to back those ideas with hard cash. A generation earlier, Lord Townshend had introduced on his neighbouring estate at Raynham the startling new concept that there was no need for the wasteful fallow year which consumed one-third of the potential space for crops. Instead of the ancient sequence of wheat, barley, fallow, he undertook a four-year cycle of wheat, turnips, barley, clover. Turnips and clover not only introduced nitrogen into the soil but could also be used for cattle-food. Thomas Coke adopted this improved sequence at Holkham.

Meanwhile, in Leicestershire, Robert Bakewell was experimenting with selective breeding of cattle. A jovial rolypoly figure, who entertained on a scale almost as lavish as Coke himself, he too freely allowed others to study his methods. By this cross-fertilization of ideas, he produced cattle and sheep which weighed anything up to three times as much as similar breeds a century earlier. His system, too, was introduced on the Holkham estate. The enormous financial yield of the estate was, in very large part, a paper transaction – for Coke ploughed back perhaps £500,000 during the 60-odd years of his regime. Some of it went to financing such unlikely experiments as marling – using the mud-like but minerally rich clay as a fertilizer. Other large sums were spent indirectly – building decent homes for his tenants and labourers, establishing a very high standard of rural housing. Coke himself habitually went about his estate dressed in an ordinary workman's smock, indistinguishable from his labourers as he worked by their side – frequently at the same humble task. In London it was said of him, grandiloquently, that he saved his country with a ploughshare where a sword would have failed. It was a true enough assessment of his contribution during the long and desperate years of the Napoleonic Wars. But his fellow East Anglians, with their own pawky sense of humour, summed up his achievement with the remark that when he took over at Holkham the only thing the estate yielded 'was one blade of grass – and two rabbits fighting for that'.

Coke was an excellent example of that very distinctive

breed of eighteenth-century aristocrats who were investigating the essence of natural forces from a sheer love of learning. But while others were examining such subjects as gas and light and air, achieving swift and dramatic results, Coke and his fellows plodded down the unglamorous path of agriculture where an experiment could take decades to produce a result. But, urban though they appeared to be, the English had never lost their almost mystic relationship with the land. 'Peasant', for them, was never a term of contempt: when they wanted such a term they had to go to a foreign language and import the word 'boor'. It was, on the whole, the norm for a landowner to get manure on his boots and mud on his hands while working the land that he owned, and this conferring of respectability upon practical farmwork goes far to explain why English farming methods soared ahead. Even poor George the Third threw himself into the English custom and received, as accolade from his subjects, the title of 'Farmer George'. Innovations spread slowly: Coke said wryly that his use of the sowing drill spread through East Anglia at the rate of one mile a year.

Theoretical publications helped to increase the speed of propagation. In 1776 appeared the first number of the *Farmer's Magazine*; it was joined by the *Farmer's Journal* in 1806, incontestable proof that there was a paying public for such publications. Arthur Young, failed farmer turned propagandist, toured the country visiting the more go-ahead landowners and reported back to his readers in a series of books that provided entertainment as well as information. William

The inter-relationship of industry and agriculture: gathering teasels for cloth-iers, 1814. Teasels were used to raise the nap on cloth

47

Cobbett clumped back and forwards, encouraging, railing, boasting, castigating, prodding. By the time Queen Victoria ascended to the throne (1837), the trauma of the enclosures was, for most, simply a fading memory. The failures were either dead, absorbed into the booming towns, or eking out some kind of life on the cold charity of the parish. Their holdings had long since disappeared, together with their scrawny cattle and their skinny pigs. The quickset hedges were now solid barriers, marching over the once open land, behind which plump cattle grazed on lush grass, wheat bore heavy ears of corn, new-fangled crops of turnips and potatoes promised plenty for winter. A transient visitor might be forgiven for thinking that the Millennium was about to dawn.

The Squirearchy

The enthusiastic fondness of the English for the country is the effect of their laws. Primogeniture is at the root of it. Scarcely any persons who hold a leading place in the circles of their society live in London. They have *houses* in London, in which they stay while Parliament sits, and occasionally visit at other seasons. But their *homes* are in the country. Their turretted mansions are there with all that denotes perpetuity – heirlooms, family memorials, pictures, tombs . . . The permanent interests and affections of the most opulent classes centre almost universally in the country. Heads of families go there to resume their stand in the midst of these feelings and all, to partake of the pastimes of country life, where they flourish in pomp and joy.

The inter-relationship of industry and agriculture: the preemer boy, 1814. His job was to detach bits of wool from the used teasel

This is a surprisingly amiable view of the English artisto-cracy considering that it came from the pen of Richard Rush, ambassador of the infant American republic. But it was an opinion shared by the Comte de Montalambert, a citizen of England's traditional enemy and an aristocrat very much aware of the causes of the bloody ruin which had overtaken his class in France. The foundation of England's stability, he thought, was that the nobility closely identified themselves with the country, source of their wealth, instead of flocking to the capital and the court. 'They did not disdain, as the old French nobility did, to accept administrative, legislative and judicial functions. Far from it, they have almost monopolized them,' he wrote – and so they exerted continuing control over the development of all England outside the great cities.

The country was still homogeneous. Society was composed of lateral slabs, graduating upwards from the labourer via the small farmer, and the gentry, to the great landowner whose estate might be run by an agent. In the absence of easy lines of communication, the lower classes identified themselves with their neighbouring superiors rather than with their equals in a distant part of the country. A Norfolk labourer on the Holkham estate had far more interests in common with the great Thomas Coke, Earl of Leicester, than with a coal-heaver in London, a fisherman in Cornwall or, for that matter, a farm labourer in Devon. And that sense of responsibility towards their inferiors which a later age was to dismiss under the term 'paternalism', was still seen as a very important duty by the landed gentry.

Describing one of these magnates, George Grenville etched what was virtually a collective portrait of the squire:

> The Duke of Rutland is as selfish as any man of his class – that is, he never does what he does not like, and spends his whole life in a round of such pleasure as suits his taste, but he is neither a foolish nor a bad man and, partly from a sense of duty and partly from inclination, he devotes time and labour on his estate.

Grenville was particularly impressed with the Duke's range of activities on behalf of the local poor. He was a guardian of a very large union, regularly attending the weekly meetings of the guardians, personally visiting the wretched paupers, noting their complaints and actually taking action to correct abuses that were brought to his notice. Perhaps the worst charge that could be laid against such a man was not a lack of compassion or goodwill, but simply a lack of imagination. He could delight in giving a splendid feast for his tenants at Christmas and perhaps on his heir's birthday, benevolently

strolling among the deferential revellers and beaming as his gallons of ale, mountains of beef and tons of plum pudding disappeared down hundreds of throats – and it would not even cross his mind to wonder what these hastily gorging people ate on the 364 or 365 other days of the year.

The eighteenth century saw the beginning of the last great wave of country-house building. The Grand Tour was still a formative influence – some dedicated seekers after culture still managed to slip abroad during the wars which dominated the century. The tourist would return, head stuffed full of the classical wonders he had seen, to find his coffers stuffed full with the gold yielded by his own unglamorous acres. This was the period which gave birth to Holkham Hall. Thomas Coke's uncle had been in Italy when he first met William Kent and became fired with the idea of transferring Rome to Norfolk. He did so some sixteen years later when Kent became his architect and designed the Hall. In the hands of a lesser man it could have been a hodgepodge, a farrago gleaned from half a dozen sources. But, in the hands of William Kent and with Coke's courteous but steely mind controlling the whole, Holkham Hall was a synthesis – with richly variegated Mediterranean origins inside and an austere exterior which was completely at home beneath the cold Norfolk skies.

Holkham, Kedleston, Kirby, Woburn, Heveningham, Syon – so the splendid tale went. In some cases new structures arose out of virgin soil, in others a modest family home turned into a palace more fitting for its owner's new wealth. It was now that landscape gardening achieved its peak. There were few men

The three faces of the country:
Above left Holkham Hall, Norfolk, seat of Thomas Coke
Centre Sign of an enlightened landlord: workman's cottage on the Holkham estate
Above right Rural slum

like Coke, who preferred to turn his mind and wealth towards turnips, pigs and wheat. Most were happy enough to have a home farm discreetly tucked away somewhere, but spent the bulk of their money on removing or raising hills, creating avenues, lakes, copses and temples.

The true life of any country district looked towards the upper levels of the gentry, rather than to the aristocracy, for a constant centre. Although the peer might be the titular land-lord, his seat could be on the other side of Britain, and his local place was taken by an agent whose main interest was the collection of rents. It was the squires who found their way into literature – Henry Fielding's Squire Weston and Squire Alworthy, Robert Surtees's Lord Scamperdale, Mrs Gaskell's Squire Hamely and Charles Dickens's Wardle – who typified the solid, enduring stratum of rural society. But the novelists tended to exaggerate and distort them, seeing them either as bucolic Father Christmases or rural tyrants. They could, perhaps, best be summed up as benevolent despots – generous to their dependents, but expecting in return total obedience and total deference. Sir John Boileau, who ruled Ketteringham in Norfolk like a lord as late as 1841, summed up in his person their contradictory qualities. His workers and tenants lived in well designed, well built houses for which they paid a low rent. They received a generous salary, and Boileau even adopted what appears to have been a sliding scale, increasing wages in times of scarcity or inflation. His wife was the classic Lady Bountiful, superintending the distribution of coal, plum pudding, beef and other necessities to the poor. But in all matters of religion, Boileau demanded total subservience to his own convictions, and was fully prepared to evict anybody who was foolish enough to advance contrary – or even different – ideas.

A little below, or to one side, of the squire (the exact position was frequently a matter of acrimonious debate) was the parson. By the late eighteenth century the fierce blaze of religious controversy had died down – certainly in the rural areas – into a mellow light. There was to be another brilliant blaze in the nineteenth century when evangelical Christianity was on the march, but at the turn of the century Christianity was virtually a code of right conduct, a means of providing a frame of social reference. The villagers who obediently trooped to church, neatly dressed and shining with soap, had no great expectation of revelation as the parson orated on the improbable exploits of obscure semitic tribes. Significantly, the anti-clericalism that in Latin countries turned the priest into a devil, in England merely turned the parson into a fool. Frequently, only too frequently, he was a member of the lower aristocracy or the gentry, a younger son who had been dispossessed by the iron law of primogeniture. A tincture of learning, together with gentlemanly manners, ensured him a not too arduous living whose returns varied enormously according to his family's influence. The English, with an unusual directness of speech, precisely defined his role and motives when they termed his sacred office a 'living'.

The living could be in the gift of the local squire, a distant peer, one of the great institutes of the state such as the Crown, the Church itself or a university college – or the parson himself. It was when squire and parson were the same person that there evolved the somewhat repulsive figure of the squarson – the hard-riding, hard-drinking, gluttonous figure of innumerable caricatures. Unsympathetic figure though he seems, the squarson probably more truly reflected the rural Englishman's approach to religion than did a more intellectual man. If the living was in the gift of a distant person or body, then the parson had reasonable freedom of action. But when the living was in the gift of the local squire, conflict frequently occurred. Even if the squire had no particular interest in religious debate, his habit of authority would lead him to exert some control over the parson's social activities at least. The parson, without a private income of sorts, was in a singularly unhappy and vulnerable position.

The bulk of the parson's income came from a tax which has been universally hated from the so-called Age of Faith through to the twentieth century – the tithe. Not until 1836 was the physical levying of a literal tenth compounded into a regular cash payment, usually computed as a percentage of land rent. Until that date, the agnostic, indifferent, or actively anti-clerical villager had the galling experience of actually choosing one-tenth of his produce – one calf in ten, one pig in ten, one bushel of wheat in ten – and taking it to the great tithe barn. The experience was probably as galling for a sensitive parson, particularly in times of shortage. But for an insensitive man, intent upon his rights, tithing could induce a squalid scene with parson and villager quarrelling over the quality of the tenth.

Once there had been a clear-cut distinction between gentry and the rest. The parson, whatever his original social background, was included with the upper class. There was then a deep and unbridgeable gap with, beyond it, the deferential small farmers, labourers and the rest. But that once clear-cut division became a twilight zone at the end of the eighteenth century and the beginning of the nineteenth, as there infiltrated into the countryside the ambiguous figures of those who had made their fortune in the towns. They joined those other ambiguous, but resident, figures – the small farmers who had suddenly made a lot of money. Surtees's fictional figure of Jorrocks, the Cockney grocer who made good and thrust his way into county circles, is almost – but not quite – the ideal example of the urban social climber. Jorrocks had made his

Farmer Giles and his wife showing off their daughter Betty: Gillray's cruel caricature of the parvenu farmer, 1809

pile; he was unabashedly buying his way into society; he was irredeemably vulgar. But he was also a very shrewd man, perfectly aware of what he was getting for his money and declining to hide his background – whereas the typical new social climber did everything possible to obscure his origins. Or at least his wife did. About twenty years after Surtees had launched his fox-hunting grocer, Anthony Trollope painted the picture of a rural social climber – the wife of a farmer who had made a modest fortune, who now sought to thrust her way among those who had once been immeasurably above her. Her husband refused to take part in the embarassing business – but the vulgar, overdressed, simpering Mrs Lookaloft and her daughters succeed, even at the cost of being cut dead by the rest of the guests at the party into which they had forced their way. Their genteel hostess deplored their presence, but had not quite the confidence to refuse them entry – a significant comment on how far rural life had changed by the 1850s.

The Rural Worker

These men, women and children who lived in the countryside, earning their living from the most ancient of skills, formed the basis of society in a very real, numerical sense. At the turn of the eighteenth century there were over $1\frac{1}{4}$ million agricultural workers, together forming the biggest single industry in Britain.

There is, however, a peculiar difficulty in identifying the life pattern of the agricultural worker at this time and in assessing the quality of that life. In the towns, a wide range of new industries was creating distinctive sub-classes of workers, each with its peculiar stresses and advantages. There was no difficulty, in the towns, in distinguishing between master and man, between the coal-heaver and the distant organizer of his labour, between the weaver and the factory owner. In the country, however, the traditional nature of farming gives an appearance of continuity, and makes it difficult to distinguish between strata at the lower levels. The man who proudly called himself an independent farmer, with the powers of hiring and firing, might very well be scratching an existence out of a few poor acres, his annual income only a few pounds more than the day-labourer he hired. In times of want he could, at least, eat his own produce – and that, perhaps, was the sum of the difference between the smaller farmers and the labourers.

Throughout the period, too, a false golden glow is shed by the frequently superficial observations of foreign travellers and predominantly urban novelists. Charles Dickens, above all, who could paint such a terrible picture of urban poverty, bears heavy responsibility for the picture-postcard view of rural life with its rosy-cheeked matrons, robust swains, plum pudding, ale and endless jollity. Mrs Gaskell and George Eliot made some attempt at reality, but not until the end of the nineteenth century, when the worst depression was in fact past, did Thomas Hardy arrive to speak for the rural worker as Dickens had spoken for the urban worker nearly a generation earlier.

The novelists were, perhaps, drawing upon the observations of travellers – particularly foreign travellers like the Frenchman Grosley. At the end of the eighteenth century he could scarcely believe the prosperity of the peasantry in England, describing their solidly built cottages, their ample, varied diet, their sturdy boots and clothes. And if the Frenchman was perhaps led in error by the barrier of the language, there was the American Louis Simond to confirm the tale. In 1810 he remarked on the almost idyllic life of the English rural labourer: 'The poor do not look as poor here as in other countries,' he thought, 'or at least poverty does not intrude on your sight and it is necessary to seek it out.' People lived well, ate well and enjoyed their limited but wholesome pleasures.

Simond's phrase, that it was necessary to 'seek out poverty', possibly provides a clue to the myopia of the traveller. In the cities, it was impossible to ignore poverty: it was ubiquitous in its stench, its cries, its appearance. In the country, poverty was likely to be hidden behind honeysuckle. Starvation was seasonal. The summertime visitor, seeing the cottage gardens generously yielding plums, apples, potatoes and cabbages, would reasonably conclude that here was a land of plenty – overlooking the fact that less than half the produce could be stored for winter and that the gardens were not large enough to feed a hungry family for a year. He would probably be staying with one or other of the local gentry and gain no closer view into the lives of the villagers than could be obtained from the back of a horse. He would see the pretty exterior of the cottage – not its damp, ill-smelling, dark, grotesquely overcrowded interior.

But side by side with the reports of a Golden Age are the terrible indictments of those who made it their business to look closer into the lives of the peasantry. In the 1790s, a little after the Frenchman Grosley had patted England on the back for the condition of her peasantry, the Englishman Sir Morton Eden assembled a devastating body of first-hand

55

'The Rivals: prize peasant versus prize pig' – agricultural conditions in 1846, as seen by Leech

evidence regarding the condition of that same peasantry. His book, *The State of the Poor,* was essentially statistical in nature. Correspondents in parishes scattered all over England and Wales provided him with detailed family budgets, covering virtually everything from the cost of a waistcoat, via coals and candle-ends, to oatmeal and bacon. Although supposed to be a general survey of the poor, the main sources for the book were derived from the family budgets of rural labourers up and down the country.

In Eden's pages occurs the story of James Strudwick, the day-labourer who was thereby immortalized, doomed to be cited again and again by the gentry as an example of how the honest and industrious poor should live. The story is told by Ann Hurst who was – significantly – his widow. She and her husband were born at about the same time early in the eighteenth century. They were both employed on the same farm and were married when she was 20. He was then earning a shilling a day – and he was still earning a shilling a day when he stopped work 60 years later, just seven days before his death at the age of 80. Never once in all those years had he had relief from the parish; never once had he had a holiday; never once had he visited the village tavern. Indeed, his widow boasted, in the whole of his life he had never spent five shillings on himself.

Ann was about 80 when her husband died – but she went out to work for herself, weeding a garden for about 6d a day. She did not consider herself ill-used. She did not think that the farmer, who had employed her husband at a fixed wage during a period of soaring prices, had any moral duty towards his widow. She had only two anxieties: that she would not be able to provide a decent funeral for James and that she should not, herself, be forced to ask for 'charity' in her last days.

The precise, passionless tones of Sir Morton Eden provide a kind of background for the emotional outbursts of the propagandists. Predominant amongst them was William Cobbett. Honesty might oblige him to admit that the enclosed fields were, in purely economic and agricultural terms, highly successful. But as for the effect on a once free peasantry: 'The labourers seem miserably poor. Their dwellings are little better than pigbeds and their looks indicate that their food is not nearly equal to that of a pig . . . And this is "prosperity", is it?' he wrote on the first of his Rides in 1821. Worse, much worse, was to come. Nine years later the Liberal Member of Parliament E. G. Wakefield was describing the condition of the agricultural worker in almost unbelievable terms:

An English agricultural labourer and an English pauper – these words are synonomous. From his earliest childhood he had bad food, and only half enough to still his hunger, and even yet he undergoes the pangs of hunger almost all the time he is not asleep. He is half clad, and has not more fire than barely suffices to cook his scanty meal. He is married, but he knows nothing of the joys of the husband and father. His wife and children – hungry, rarely warm, often ill and helpless, always careworn and hopeless like himself – are naturally grasping, selfish and troublesome and so, to use his own expression, he hates the sight of them and enters his cot only because it offers him a trifle more shelter from wind and rain than a hedge. His abject and submissive demeanour towards his wealthy neighbours shows that they treat him roughly and with suspicion, hence he fears and hates them but he will never injure them by force . . . His wretched existence is brief: rheumatism and asthma bring him to the workhouse where he will draw his last breath without a single pleasant recollection.

Powerful words – overdrawn, exaggerated, redolent of party political warfare, but conveying the feeling of a terrible truth. The spate of enclosures did not bring some Golden Age suddenly to an end. There were landless paupers long before the eighteenth century. Nevertheless, the beginning of the spectacular decline of the rural labourer coincides with the period of mass enclosure.

It was as though a hairbreadth fracture in rural society was spreading. Amongst the earlier evidence of change was the ending of that ancient system in which a young, unmarried man lived with his master, virtually as part of the family. His wages were low – £5 or £6 a year – and paid yearly so that it was virtually impossible for him to break with his master without permission. But his food was good and certain: 'the old oak table, spread in the homely farmhouse for the farmer and his family – wife, children, servants male and female, is heaped with the rude plenty of beans and bacon, beef and cabbage, fried potatoes and bread,' was how William Howitt nostalgically described the huge communal meals. He slept rough – but no rougher than in his father's cottage and at least with companions of his own age and tastes. He worked hard, literally from dawn to dusk six days a week. But so did his father who, at the end of his working day, had to turn to and make do and mend. And at the end of his time, when he came to marry, the young man would have a nest egg and his master would make him the present, perhaps, of a sow in farrow. Even after he had set up home there would be largesse and eggs, for he would be regarded simply as 'living out'.

The greatly increased size of the new farms put an end to this practice. It did not happen simultaneously all over the country: rather was it a gradual withering away, the more remote areas continuing the custom until late in the nineteenth century. The reason for discontinuing was partly economic, partly social: larger farms required more labourers and there was just not enough room for them at the communal table. But could not that table be, perhaps, enlarged? Theoretically, there was no reason why not. In practice, the farmer's wife regarded it as beneath her new-found dignity to preside over a table where clodhopping employees rubbed shoulders with her own children. Her daughters, granted a brief glimpse into the daily life of the upper classes, found it intolerable that they should breathe the same air indoors as an uncouth yokel from the village. The yokel was accordingly banished to his father's cottage.

William Howitt, who usually tried to put a good face on conditions in the countryside, cannot be accused of exaggerating when he described the interior of a labourer's cottage: 'There is his tenement of, at most, one or two rooms. His naked walls, bare brick, stone or mud floor, as it may be: a few wooden or rush-bottomed chairs: a deal or old oak table: a simple fireplace with its oven beside it or, in many parts of the kingdom, no other fireplace than the hearth: a few pots and pans and you have his whole abode, goods and chattels.'

A farm labourer's working life started literally as soon as he could walk. From scaring birds, gleaning corn or potatoes, gathering berries and fungi, or anything wild that could possibly be turned into food for the family, the child graduated to earning a few pennies by helping to drive cattle, wandering miles from home. At harvest time, boys and girls alike worked from dawn to dusk, adding a few pence each week to the few pathetic shillings that their father brought home. Precious little of their potential earning time was used up by schooling. Here and there throughout the country a few philanthropists set up village schools – and met suspicion and insult for their pains. It was, perhaps, natural that an illiterate parent should resent the loss of a child's earning capacity while it was engaged in a seemingly nonsensical activity. But others who should have known better were just as vehemently against the system. Cobbett, for one, condemned it outright, swearing that 'nothing is taught but the rudiments of servility, pauperism and slavery'. Work was the only true education – that was how the vast majority, gentry and proletariat, viewed the subject. Throughout the whole of this climacteric period, when Western

Gathering outside a country inn, from the painting by Luke Clennell (1781–1840)

58

Europe was poised on the edge of the most dizzying flight ever essayed by man, the education of the majority of Britain's children was probably lower than it had been during the Dark Ages.

Wages had risen slowly, in reluctant response to the general rise in the cost of living. They varied greatly over the country, reflecting for the most part the efficiency of farming in a given locality. Thus in Dorset, in 1795, labourers were still getting a shilling a day, rising to 18 pence at harvest time. But in Norfolk the standard daily rate was 18 pence and in Lincolnshire it rose to a princely 2 shillings for such skilled workers as ploughmen. Labourers working in these areas, and on the more efficient and larger farms elsewhere, could count on regular work almost throughout the year. Elsewhere, they were obliged to endure the humiliation of the daily hiring, grouping together outside the village inn to be inspected by the local farmers. The hard-working, willing men scarcely put in a token appearance before being engaged. The 'difficult' man, or one in poor health, could attend fruitlessly day after day – in particular during the dead period. Nothing was more demoralizing than that sickening realization, sometime after the sun rose, that nothing but an empty day lay ahead. Small wonder that the man would slouch into the tavern, if he had the price of a drink on him, rather than return to his hovel and the accusing, reproachful or simply terrified eyes of his wife.

Until the industrialization of cottage industries, most rural workers had these, at least, to fall back on in times of hardship. Indeed, in some areas – notably the weaving districts of Yorkshire – this 'secondary' industry took precedence over the rural worker's nominal trade of farm-labourer, and continued to do so until the mid-nineteenth century. 'They have looms in their houses, and unite the business of weavers and farmers', an observer noted in the West Riding in 1851. 'When trade is good the farm is neglected: when trade is dull, the weaver becomes a more attentive farmer. His holding is generally under twenty acres and his chief stock consists of dairy cows.' In the writer's opinion, such union of trades was inefficient and the land that the weaver-farmer occupied 'is believed to be the worst managed in the district'. Nevertheless, it did provide him with milk and potatoes when trade was slack, and the loom gave him a little gold in times of agricultural depression. But elsewhere in the country this lifeline had long since departed. Weaving was the major secondary occupation, but there were also many little trades such as fancy-box making, fan-making and the like which once had brought in a few

'The Crow-boy's Christmas Lunch'. The accompanying poem suggested that the lad was agog with delight because he had an extra slice of cheese. An urban, middle-class view of the peasant

59

pence. But the great monster of steam-power did not disdain even these flimsy, frivolous manufactures and one more source of income was permanently lost to the farm-worker's family.

The Napoleonic Wars drastically altered the basis of rural economy. In the 1770s the average price of wheat was around 50s a quarter; in the 1790s the price began to soar, rising to an astonishing 100 shillings a quarter before the Battle of Waterloo in June 1815. This was the period when the farmer's wife decked herself and her daughters in fashionable new garments; when the smaller gentry filled their houses with kickshaws; when the aristocracy pulled down their modest Elizabethan or medieval manor houses and built great palaces. And this was the period, too, when the labourer learned to eat meat sometimes twice a week, and could afford a few pence to experiment with that curious new drink, made of dried infused leaves, that had been all the rage with the gentry a decade or so earlier. Then came the great agricultural crash, when wheat sank from an all-time high of 106s a quarter to the catastrophic level of 66s. All strata of rural society were affected but, inevitably, it was the lowest stratum that bore the heaviest blows. The aristocrat had the revenue of his mines to fall back on. The squire could cut down on some of his family's extravagances. The labourer simply took a cut in pay – and he had to fight desperately to keep what remained. With Napoleon safe on St Helena, a grateful country was discharging as fast as it could the soldiers that had brought Boney to his knees. The army that had faced the Old Guard at Waterloo had been predominantly drawn from the rural areas of England. The men returned now to scrabble for a living, competing directly with their stay-at-home brothers. In the peaceful vales of England the materials for revolution were being piled as high as they were in the teeming cities.

Idealized views of the country:
Right A detail from 'The Reapers', by George Stubbs
Opposite An eighteenth-century jug showing villagers merrymaking in an idyllic landscape

3 The Complex Automaton

Coal-mining

Hindsight delights in imposing patterns, detecting causes and assigning effects, in relating together what seemed to be wholly disparate elements. And hindsight is, usually, accurate – from a height and at a distance, we are able to perceive relationships which are perhaps wholly obscured to those unconsciously creating them, or being affected by them. Occasionally, however, there occurs some complex phenomenon whose inter-relationship remains as mysterious to posterity as it was unknown or obscure to contemporaneity. The Neolithic Revolution, the Renaissance, the voyages of discovery – each displayed the same characteristic, the apparently spontaneous and simultaneous emerging of skills and discovery of materials, each of which depended upon the existence of the other. A similar phenomenon happened in Britain in the late eighteenth century, and of all its components the most mysterious relationship was that between the three industries which made all else possible – coal, steam and iron. Without coal, there would have been no steam; without steam, coal production would have remained at a primitive level; without iron, the power of steam could not have been used to raise the level of coal production. But without coal, the quality and quantity of iron would have been far below the demands made of it. Progress had to be virtually simultaneous in each of the three industries in order to stimulate

64

advance in all.

At the beginning of the eighteenth century, the three industries were wholly unrelated. The enormous energy locked up in air pressure had been known since the days of Classical Greece, but it was still a toy for the scientifically minded aristocrat. The use of iron was very nearly as old as civilization – and so was the technique still used to produce it. And the citizens of Georgian England mined coal in much the same way as their Neolithic ancestors had mined flints. However, if any one of the three elements can be identified as the prime cause of change in the others, it would be coal-mining.

There is no clearer indication of the altered direction that civilization was taking than in the figures for coal production in Britain between 1700 and 1850. In 1700 production was some 3 million tons a year, a little over double the production of a century earlier. By 1800, production had more than trebled to 11 million tons and was still soaring. It doubled to 23 million tons by 1830 and doubled yet again to 49 million tons by the end of the period.

For centuries, coal-mining had been little more than a branch of farming, one of the secondary industries to which the small independent farmer could turn when the pressing business of sowing or harvesting had been accomplished. The mine, indeed, could not have operated without the farm, for stabling and forage was needed for the horses who worked at the pit. Except in the north-east, where the proximity of coalfields to the coast allowed coal to be shipped in bulk, output was for local purposes, supplementing the use of timber. But as the industrial demand for fuel began to move upward and to outstrip traditional supplies, so the mines were sunk

Pre-industrial power: charcoal burners, 1807. Dwindling supplies of wood provided a powerful impetus for the development of coal-mines

deeper, the internal arrangements becoming more elaborate and the problems to be solved ever more complex.

The actual cutting out of the coal – the attack upon the solid coalface running like a wall below ground – was, and remained, a matter of sheer animal strength until the very end of the nineteenth century. Pick and crowbar were the basic tools wielded by men crouching, kneeling or even lying in painfully contorted positions. Apart from muscle-power, the only additional energy employed in the front-line position was the use of blasting powder for opening up new positions – a hazardous business until the invention of the safety fuse in 1831. A major preoccupation was ensuring that the roof held up long enough to extract all accessible coal in the vicinity. In the shallower mines – those not more than 900 feet deep – this could be achieved by leaving massive pillars of coal 30 feet or more thick. After the area around them had been cleared, slices were taken off the pillars and wooden props inserted as the natural supports became thinner and thinner. In the deeper mines, the immense pressure would have simply squashed both the coal pillars and the wooden supports: there, the technique was to hew out the coal in one swift operation, taking in a width of not less than 100 yards at a time but only a few feet deep, and hastily erecting pillars of stone as the cut advanced.

Children being lowered down a mine shaft: from the 1842 Report of the Royal Commission which investigated working conditions in mines and factories

The transportation of coal from the face to the pit-head was, again, for decades, a business of sheer brute force, and here it was that an ancient human custom produced a modern and most inhuman result. The miners at the coalface belonged to a tradition in which the family's living was earned by the family as a whole. The man, naturally, worked at his trade full-time – whether it was as weaver, farm-labourer or baker – but his wife and children contributed their labour according to their strength and skill. There could be little objection on grounds of physical well-being if the child or woman was called upon to make hay, scare birds, spin wool, carry loaves or whatever ancillary task was required to keep the main breadwinner fully occupied. But when this same concept of family assistance was transferred to the deep mines, inhumanity resulted. The miner's task was to cut coal, and he would be lowering his earning capacity if he, personally, had to transfer the cut coal to the pit-head. It therefore made economic sense for his wife and children to undertake the task.

But, arguably, that task demanded an output of muscular energy almost as great as that needed to hew the coal out from the face. Until the invention of the 'railway' underground, coal was loaded into wicker baskets and dragged on sledges. Apart from the dragging friction between the sledge and the rough ground, the tunnels were so low that it was impossible to walk upright and so throw the full weight of the body against the harness. In many tunnels, indeed, women and children had to crawl on hands and knees, and grotesquely calloused knees were a mark of the trade. But even on arrival at the shaft the worst was by no means over, for the only access to the outside world was up a series of ladders. Laden with the dead-weight of the coal baskets, the women and older children clambered steep ladders. At the top, frequently weeping with fatigue, they had just as long to rest as it took to empty the basket before they turned and clambered down into the pitch-black, choking hell of the mine. Horse-gins were used in many pits to supplement or replace this human labour, but until the advent of steam-power in the early nineteenth century, a very large proportion of those 11 million tons of coal produced annually was carted up from the depths on the trembling back of a human beast of burden, usually female, frequently immature. Even after pit-ponies began to be used underground around the 1760s, humans were still employed to drag coal along tunnels that were too low for the animals. By then, however, rails had been laid and wagons with wheels moved smoothly along them – an innovation that ranked with the greatest of social reforms as far as the two-legged beast was concerned.

As the mines went deeper and the tunnels travelled even further from the shaft, so the problem of ventilation, light and flood became ever more acute. At the greater depths, the danger of explosion loomed far larger – in particular, explosion caused by the methane gas released during the mining operations. One of the riskiest jobs in the mine was that of the fireman, whose task was to ignite the gas before it achieved dangerous proportions. His equipment was simple – wet sacks to cover his body and head and a candle at the end of a long pole. If he was lucky, the amount of gas that his lighted candle encountered would produce only a small, local explosion. If he was unlucky, he, and the waiting miners behind him, risked death or severe injury.

Under these circumstances, the use of naked lights underground was out of the question. Some miners made use, bizarrely, of decomposing fish-skin: this gave off a phosphorescent glow which allowed at least a simple orientation. In the mid-eighteenth century the flint-and-steel mill appeared. As the mill was turned against the flint it produced a continu-

Fireman at work in a mine: a lonely and dangerous job

ous shower of sparks which not only shed light, but also acted as an indicator of the presence of explosive gas – the sparks grew larger and more luminous when gas was about. But despite such crude safety precautions, as the mines went deeper so the frequency and destructiveness of explosions increased. In 1813, the Sunderland Society was formed in an attempt to reduce the appalling death toll. A direct result of the society's existence was the invention of the safety lamp. Humphry Davy has gone down in history as the man who, in the thankful words of one mining engineer, 'subdued this monster' – but he was only one of several inventors of a workable safety lamp. Another was George Stephenson, the practical engineer. Davy's invention, however, was significant in that it was the product of laboratory rather than workshop, an early and vivid example of the application of science to technology. To his credit, he refused any financial reward from an invention which could have earned him a small fortune – a gesture gracefully returned by the mine owners of Newcastle when they subscribed to a gift of plate for him.

The problem of ventilation was solved by using the elemental power of fire. The obvious source of ventilation was via the main shaft. A furnace installed there drew air from the interior of the mine and expelled it upwards and outwards. The sinking of a second shaft was a natural development which not only increased the flow of purer air, but also acted as an emergency exit. But again a social outrage was created as by-product of a technical need. The current of air was directed to the areas where it was required by the opening or closing of trapdoors in the tunnels. Coal trams, too, needed to pass through the trapdoors and a device was needed to open and close the doors as required. The device was installed – a small child seated near the trapdoor and given simple instructions to pull this or push that as need be. Little strength was required to operate the trapdoors and, as small children cost marginally less than large children, one more class of victim was accordingly fed to the Moloch that was producing the world's first industrial society. Boys or girls of perhaps five years old were left in total darkness for hour after hour, quite alone except when some human beast laboured by, pulling or pushing the coal train. It is difficult to imagine what the child feared more than the terror and boredom engendered by the endless black hours.

At least two generations of women and children were consumed down the deep mines in the task of transporting coal from face to pit-head. They were released not through any spasm of conscience, but by an enormous force that was conjured up for a wholly different purpose. Steam-power was first employed in the mines to solve the problem of flooding: only later was the vast power of that genie adapted to haul weights from one point to another and, by improving ventilation, release at least one class of child from a dreary vigil.

Steam-power

For centuries, wind and water had been the only non-animal source of power. But for centuries, civilized men had known of the titanic energies locked up in that ocean of air which weighed upon all created things. In the sixth century BC Anaximenes stumbled on a half truth when he propounded that fire was a rarified form of air which, when condensed, formed water and earth. Anaxegoras took the idea a stage further and daringly postulated the concept of vacuum. Sometime in the first century AD Hero of Alexandria turned theory into practice, though only for amusement, when he made his toys of atmospheric power – his 'sphere of Aeolus' which whirled merrily round, his fountain which worked on air pressure, and his fire-engine. As with so much else the

The unprecedented growth of industry created the 'Black Country' shown in this engraving of 1869

knowledge was forgotten or rejected in favour of religious disputation, during the long dark night that followed the break-up of the Roman Empire. The seventeenth century picked up the story again. In 1644 the Italian Torricelli trudged to the top of a high mountain and observed, without surprise, how the mercury in his crude barometer fell, thus proving that air indeed had weight which diminished as one rose higher. Three years later the German von Guerick harnessed his teams of horses to two halves of a sphere out of which all air had been pumped, and earned cries of wonder as the labouring beasts attempted in vain to pull the hemispheres apart. He took the whole concept an immense step nearer practical use when he built piston and cylinder, and showed

The mythical King Lud, disguised as a woman

alike that a movement which spread throughout the Midlands and the north and which, after the outbreak in Leeds, seemed to be co-ordinated like a military action, should not have a single, baleful head. The official belief was substantiated by the habit adopted by the local revolutionary committees of addressing their warnings and complaints in the name of 'General Lud'.

There was only one power wealthy enough, close enough and inimical enough to mount and maintain a military conspiracy of this nature. The war with Napoleon was approaching its bitter climax: for nearly two decades the shadow of Boney had stretched across the country and a war-wearied people had little difficulty in identifying this social upheaval with the arch-enemy. Some claimed to believe that the rebellious stockingers had simply made common cause with Napoleon, preferring a distant racial enemy to a close social enemy. It was a natural conclusion for a fearful middle class

Number 4 of five cartoons illustrating 'The Life of a Labourer', 1830: in ignorance of true causes he wrecks machinery

to reach: the workers, in their canon, had already rejected God and it was inevitable that they would now reject their country. There was no lack of gaudy rumours to give colour to the theory. The ubiquitous 'French spy', with his sallow face and thick accent, now appeared with a specific role. Stories circulated that the Luddites were receiving the handsome sum of 18 shillings a week for their subversive activities and that the disruption was costing Napoleon over £4,000 a week.

The conclusion of the war brought the 'conspiracy' theory to a natural end, for the destruction continued. In its place there developed another myth: that the Luddites were a species of simpleton who were pitting their puny wills against the giant strength of Industry itself, in a desperate attempt to turn the clock back by destroying machinery before it destroyed them. The theory was attractively simple, but curiously overlooked the fact that the stocking frame upon which the stockingers were venting their corporate rage was an Elizabethan invention and had been in widespread use for nearly 200 years.

The disciplined nature of the Luddite attacks made it clear that they were selective in their targets – considering either the nature of the machine they attacked or the character of the man who owned it. The prime target among the machines were the so-called 'wide' frames which, originally designed to knit pantaloons, were turned to the production of low-grade stockings when the European market was closed by Napoleon. Among the employers, the victims tended to be any man who paid below the accepted rate.

The initial driving force in the Luddite movement was essentially economic. There had been four bad harvests in succession – in October 1811 the wheat was still green. At the same time, Napoleon imposed a ban on all British-made goods destined for the Continent, and a similar American ban closed the valuable North American market. Soon, one in four stockingers was unemployed and the rest were forced to take heavy cuts in wages – all at a time of steeply rising prices.

But though the first impetus of the movement was economic, it continued for social reasons. At its peak, the movement affected all the Midlands and the north: hundreds were directly involved and thousands knew the identity of those taking part. Yet despite offers of rewards which amounted to more than a labourer could earn in two years, the authorities received little assistance from the common people. And not only the common people, it seemed. General Maitland, a military co-ordinator of the measures against the Luddites, openly raised the question that members of the gentry might be leading the rebellion. The letters from 'General Lud' were certainly too grammatical and too neatly written to be the product of an unschooled artisan. It seemed, too, unthinkable that members of the lower orders had the intelligence to organize military activities for such long periods and on such a scale. Money was coming in, regularly and in fairly large quantities, from some outside source. The first wave of machine-breaking – undertaken by hundreds of men – was quite certainly spontaneous. Over the following six years, however, it became equally certain that the spearhead of the movement was composed of a comparatively small number of men who were paid for their work of destruction.

The search began for a leader. Baleful eyes fell on Gravenor Henson, the Nottingham stockinger who was the recognized leader of working-class protest in the city. Later, he became the first full-time trade union organizer – at a time when trade unions were still illegal and viewed by authority with almost the same loathing as Luddism itself. No proof was ever forthcoming that Henson was closely associated with the Luddites. He may have simply been skilful in covering his tracks: more likely he was dismayed by the violent direction the stockingers had taken and voiced his opinion that Luddism was, in fact, the work of government *provocateurs*. Reformers, radical or otherwise, were inevitably suspected of Luddite sympathies or even Luddite actions – Cobbett, Cartwright and even Sir Francis Burdett were obliged to defend themselves from the charge that they were directly involved.

The threat of transportation had no effect upon the movement and so Parliament turned to the ultimate sanction – the death penalty for machine-breaking. Young Lord Byron devoted his maiden speech in the House of Lords to a vivid and generous defence of his fellow countrymen: 'I have seen them meagre with famine, sullen with despair, careless of a life which your lordships are perhaps about to value at something less than the price of a stocking-frame.' Their lordships remained unmoved: the Bill was passed and a number of working-class leaders duly choked out their lives on the end of a rope.

Luddism had come to a natural end by 1817. The stockingers had obtained what they wanted – a higher rate of pay. Indifferent to the larger political and economic picture, they were content to subside into the background again, confounding the pundits who had regarded them as the heralds of destruction. But scarcely had King Lud, mysterious lord of

Rick-burning in Kent, about 1830

urban misrule, stalked off the stage, than the equally mysterious Captain Swing, lord of rural destruction, made his entrance.

There was no mistaking the cause of the rural rebellion that culminated in the great uprising of 1830. Despair was the spur: the despair of men caught in an incomprehensible economic web and betrayed, as they thought it, by those whom they had been taught to regard as their natural leaders. The actual Swing riots began with the breaking of threshing machines – a far more logical action than the Luddite tactics, for the threshing machines demonstrably stole from a man the two or three months' work which once used to tide him over the winter. But the cause lay deeper, and further back in time, than even this logical reaction of men against machines. It lay in the break-up of what had once been a homogenous society, a break-up summed up in the bitter testimony of a farm labourer who had been called before one of the endless commissions of inquiry into the Poor Laws. He recalled how, in his childhood, master and men used to eat together in the farmhouse, the farmer's dining room and the servants' hall connecting with each other, 'and everything was carried from one table to another. Now they will rarely permit a man to live in their houses and all idea of affection is destroyed.'

The clearest indication of the new society, in which all affection was destroyed, lay in the operation of the game laws. The taking of game had always been rigorously controlled: an Act of 1671 limited it to landowners worth £100 and more. During the eighteenth century, however, the game laws achieved an almost Norman ferocity: 32 were passed during the reign of George III, each designed to close a gap, to hem in a seething populace tighter and tighter. Those who suffered most were the poor, whose only source of protein was the occasional rabbit or partridge. But the smaller tenant farmers, the smallholders owning less than £100, suffered a greater frustration and humiliation. The lands they farmed might be swarming with game and their tender green crops devoured by rabbits. But they were forbidden to touch a single animal, under pain of a fine of £5 for each head of game. Poaching became commonplace, with the tenant farmers turning a blind eye. The landowners reacted by increasing the number of gamekeepers: the poachers took to working by night. The landowners pushed an Act through Parliament which imposed six months' imprisonment on anyone caught poaching between sunset and sunrise; the poachers replied by organizing themselves into gangs.

From this moment on, the conflict escalated in savagery –

the poachers became ever more merciless and Parliament, manipulated by and for the landowners, obligingly passed ever fiercer penalties, culminating in the Ellenborough Act of 1803 which decreed the death penalty for any poacher offering armed resistance to arrest. The ending of the Napoleonic Wars, which flooded the countryside with thousands of tough veterans, coupled with the disastrous increase in food prices, stepped up the tempo of the conflict. Hitherto, apart from the very poor, the poachers had entered into their work partly in a spirit of braggadocio and partly because they were attracted by the very high prices that game fetched in the black market. Now, however, their ranks were augmented by men for whom poaching was the only means of providing food for their families. Again, Parliament stepped up the penalties, decreeing seven years' transportation for anyone caught poaching even with a net. For a desperate man, transportation appeared as little more than a protracted death sentence for his wife and children. They had scarcely the means of subsistence even with him to provide for them: how would they fare when he was thousands of miles away with little hope of ever returning? The man who had once hesitated to carry a weapon now weighed the chances of being recognized by a gamekeeper against the chances of being hanged for resisting arrest, and only too often joined the violent and the near-criminal.

> this is to inform you what you have to undergo Jentelmen if
> providing you won't pull down your messhenes and rise the
> poor mens wages the maried men give tow and sixpence a day a
> day the singel tow shillings or we will burn down your barns and
> you in them this is the last notis

So ran a typical letter from 'Captain Swing'. The most obvious difference between him and his urban counterpart, King Lud, was his comparative illiteracy. In addition, he lacked the virtually military control over his followers which had enabled King Lud to plan attacks miles apart, complete with diversionary tactics. Finally, his origins were even more mysterious than King Lud's. He did not even possess that tenuous link with a real person which gave young Ned Ludlam his niche in history. There was never any doubt but that 'Captain Swing' was a purely mythical figure, the embodiment of the despair of tens of thousands of farm labourers.

Rural unrest had taken violent form as early as 1816. The weather in that first year after the Napoleonic Wars was appalling. Hunger stalked the land and, in East Anglia, a band of some hundreds of labourers went on the rampage –

'State of the Country': machine-wreckers and rick-burners, from a cartoon of 1831

firing ricks, breaking machines and demanding wage increases. No-one was killed in that violence, but the magistrates acted with brutal efficiency – hanging five of the rioters, imprisoning and transporting some scores more. Sporadic rebellions in the following years were met with equally draconic measures, including the passing of an Act which decreed transportation for machine-breaking and death for rick-burning. In June 1830, the 'Swing riots' began with an outbreak of rick-burning in Kent. This was followed by a wave of machine-smashing in the same county and then, like a burning brand dragged across the face of the country, 'Captain Swing' was on the march from Norfolk to Northampton, from Surrey to Dorset.

In her book *Our Village*, Mary Mitford described from a personal viewpoint the reaction of the gentry to the riots. It seemed to them that the bloodstained spectre of revolution had at last crossed the Channel and had taken England in its grip:

> Not an hour passed but, from some quarter or other, reports came pouring in of mobs gathering, mobs assembled, mobs marching upon us. Now the high-roads were blocked by the rioters, travellers murdered, soldiers defeated and the magistrates, who had gone out to meet and harangue them, themselves surrounded and taken by the desperate multitude. Now the artisans had risen to join the peasantry, driving out the gentry and tradespeople, while they took possession of their houses and property.

Faithfully, if with tongue in cheek, she went on to record the ever more dramatic and exaggerated rumours, 'the market place running with blood, the town hall piled with dead bodies' – all of which always took place in some other locality. She painted a vivid picture of bumbling officialdom and the arrogance of men granted brief authority – petty officials 'who, every hour, to prove their vigilance, sent in some poor wretch, beggar or match-seller, or rambling child, under denomination of suspicious person'. There was the enjoyable frisson of

In 'The Home of the Rick-Burner', *Punch* captures the sheer despair and helpless rage that could drive a labourer to rick-burning

danger, the pleasure of experiencing a break in the rural monotony, as friends and neighbours and relatives hastened from house to house of others of their class, bearing the latest rumour, ostentatiously looking to their arms. And, in a passage of considerable power, she described how:

> With the approach of night came fresh sorrows – the red glow of fires gleaming on the horizon and mounting into the middle sky: the tolling of bells and the rumbling sound of the [fire] engines clattering along from place to place and often, too often, rendered useless by the cutting of the pipes after they had begun to play . . . Oh, the horror of these fires, breaking forth night after night, sudden yet unexpected, always seeming nearer than they actually were and always said to have been more mischievous to life and property than they actually had been.

Mary Mitford's description of the horror in which arson was held helps to explain Parliament's decision to impose the death penalty for it. A complex myth arose around the whole business of rick-burning. Usually, an elaborate tale was told of how mysterious strangers were spotted on their arrival in a village where they would question the inhabitants closely about the habits and locations of the gentry. In the myth, the incendiary device was no vulgar torch but a mysterious object, fitted with a kind of timing mechanism that allowed the arsonists to be safely on their way before the flames rose up. Allied to the stories of fire-raising were tales of murder, of beating, of cattle-maiming and strangling.

The rioters, in fact, were in the main singularly gentle and unbloodthirsty rebels. The hated overseers of the poor could count on a ducking, or forcible expulsion, from villages where 'Captain Swing' gained control. But no life was lost, very little personal assault took place, and the destruction of property was limited to machine-breaking and rick-burning. In their machine-breaking, the rioters found a surprising ally in the tenant farmers. Many of them promised simply to refrain from using their threshing machines. Some actually destroyed them at the request of the local 'Captain Swing' while others agreed to raise wages to the modest level demanded by the 'rebels'. These smaller farmers were, perhaps, too close to the peasantry to be blind to their very real troubles. Above the tenant farmers were the landowners, a class distinct from farmer and labourer alike. There were excellent grounds for the suspicion that, in many villages, the destruction of some great landowner's property was done with the active assistance of a local farmer.

Don't be alarmed Gaffer, he's the only man to give these fellows an answer.

By the autumn of 1830 the major impetus of the riots had spent itself. Now authority could take revenge for the fright it had received from 'Captain Swing'. Hundreds of labourers were arrested and special commissions went into action to purge the land of the Jacobin spectre. To be accused was virtually the same as being condemned: of the hundreds tried, very few indeed went free. Nineteen were hanged – for an 'uprising' in which no person's life had been lost – and over 500 were transported, while some 700 were jailed.

The Battle for Reform

Some 15 years after Napoleon set reluctant foot upon St Helena and so marked Britain's brilliant military triumph; a generation after James Watt had tamed the titanic power of steam, and Thomas Telford had cleared the arteries of the country, and young Coke had shown how two blades of wheat could grow where once there had been a single stunted blade, Britain was slumped in a stagnant despondency. Profits were declining. The flood of artefacts produced so prodigally by the new industrial processes was clogging up the warehouses. Real income was declining along with profits – for the first time in well over a century. And, as counterpart to the roar of burning ricks in the country, a sullen silence fell over the factories in the cities as factory workers, still unorganized, discovered their most potent weapon – the strike.

The majority of urban and rural workers were, for the most part, interested only in short-term gains – an additional sixpence a day, a marginal reduction in the hours of work. But, working like a leaven throughout the whole country was the growing awareness that an industrial, urban and essentially democratic society was being run as though it were still the agricultural, rural and essentially aristocratic society it had been a century earlier. The clearest indication of this was the grotesque imbalance of parliamentary representation. The booming cities of the north, many of which had been little more than hamlets in the mid-eighteenth century, had little or no representation in the House of Commons – even though they were now immensely important centres of population. Conversely, areas from which the population had long since departed still had the power to return Members. Old Sarum, for example, once the site of Salisbury but now simply an open hill, returned two Members to Parliament. And the owner of Gatton Park in Surrey had in his pocket votes which could return himself and a friend as Members for the six houses that now comprised the Park.

Parliamentary reform as a burning social issue, and not simply an academic discussion, already had its martyrs. In Manchester in 1819, a crowd several thousand strong, gathered near St Peter's Church to hear speeches, was set upon by the militia. 500 were injured and 11 were killed – the incident became known as 'Peterloo', an ironic comment on the recent British victory at Waterloo. Some of the militia, it was observed, were wearing medals won at that famous victory. Nevertheless, it was their lack of discipline that led to the tragedy, together with the hatred of a settled, solid middle class for the 'mob' bent on introducing French revolutionary manners into Britain.

A hostile middle- and upper-class view of the growing trade union movement

Peterloo became the pretext to clamp down on the seething cauldron of reform. But drastic curtailment of the freedom of the press, the rights of assembly and free speech merely dammed and canalized an immensely powerful current that was now running through all classes, not merely a sullen urban proletariat or aridly academic theoreticians. The caricaturist George Cruikshank turned his corrosive pen on the 'borough-mongers' who, in his stark cartoon, gorged themselves at the trough crying: 'The system works well, why should it be altered?' The bloodless 1830 revolution in France, when the Bourbon King Charles X was contemptuously dismissed from the throne, gave added stimulus. And the death of the now wholly grotesque George IV provided the opportunity – for the law decreed that an election must be held within six months of the death of the monarch, and George's brother and successor, William IV, was an honest man, unskilled in the ways of politicians. He liked to be known as the 'sailor king' and was a

The Reform Parliament of 1832–3

'bursting, bubbling old gentleman, with quarter-deck gestures, round rolling eyes and a head like a pineapple'. There seemed grounds for hope that he might be steered into the current of reform. But, in the end, Sailor Bill could prove true only to his class. His speech from the throne in November 1830 ignored the bubbling discontent in the land, save only to castigate the rioting farm labourers, promising the severest penalties for their wickedness. And later on that same day his Prime Minister, the Iron Duke himself, made devastatingly clear that bravery and skill on the battlefields did not guarantee commonsense in the halls of government. Privately, Wellington had already disburdened himself of the opinion that the only way to ensure that the government continued to be run by gentlemen was to ensure the continuance of the pocket and rotten boroughs. In public now, in the House of Lords, he informed a somewhat startled nation that the British system of government was as perfect as fallible man could make it, and that any attempt at change or reform could only be for the worse: 'As far as I am concerned, as long as I hold any station in the government of the country, I shall always feel it my duty to resist such measures.'

Just 18 months after this brave declaration of intent, the First Reform Bill became law. It was not under Wellington's aegis that the first, tentative restructuring of the country took place. On the contrary, he held up his hands in horror, lamenting like some elder Prophet: 'The barriers of the constitution are broken down: the waters of destruction have burst

Part of the Chartist procession at Blackfriars, 1848

the gates of the temple.' During those 18 months the current of reform had grown muddy and wild, becoming almost the current of revolution. There were riots and there were deaths – although these were generally the result of accident. The Bill had been forced through only under the King's threat of creating so many peers that they could swamp all opposition. Wellington's fears were as exaggerated as the hopes of tens of thousands of working men, who had welcomed the support of the gentry only to see one set of rulers replaced by another. Less than 250,000 additional voters had been added to the register. Even now, only one adult male in six had the right to vote – and that male was never likely to be a factory worker or farm labourer since the qualification for voting was the possession of property rated at at least £10 a year. During the next 15 years unrest increased, culminating in the menacing year of 1848 when a vast Chartist demonstration was planned to march on London. Wellington, again cast in the role of national hero and saviour, prepared to throw 200,000 auxiliary policemen into the expected street battle. The march flickered out in humiliation and defeat, the leaders tamely agreeing to carry their monster petition by hansom cab. Superficially, the immemorial pattern of Britain continued unchanged into the second half of the nineteenth century. But, like a hair-line crack in a great dam, the Reform Bill of 1832 had begun a process of disintegration out of which a new society could be built.

159

Epilogue:
The Great Exhibition

By the middle of the nineteenth century, the country had achieved a rough equilibrium. The black days of Captain Swing and King Lud, and of reform riots and hunger, were in the past. In place of the raw clash between the haves and the have-nots, between the established upper classes and an emergent, vigorous, resentful urban working class, there was the beginning of co-operation. It was hesitant, heavily qualified, the reforms from above dictated as much by economic necessity and political fear as from any sense of abstract justice, but it was a leaven in the lump. Epitomatic was the repeal of the Corn Laws in 1846, a date which was to join 1066 and 1588 as cornerstones in innumerable textbooks. The Corn Law imposed in 1815 was, essentially, designed to protect the landed classes: foreign corn could not be imported until homegrown wheat had reached the very high level of 80s a quarter. The repeal of this artificial protection marked that moment in the country's history when the balance of power began to shift towards the urban population, away from the landed gentry. The factory owners wanted to keep their wages bill down and therefore wholeheartedly supported a measure which would reduce the price of bread, and the repeal went through despite the anguished cries of the landed classes that such a measure spelled ruin for English agriculture.

The Public Health Act of 1848, the Ten-Hour Factory Act of 1847, the spontaneous growth of the Mechanics' Institutes – all were products of the need to contain the urban explosion, to absorb the Industrial Revolution into the body of society.

The Mechanics' Institute movement that began in the 1820s was a poignant reaction among working men, anxious – almost desperate – to understand the changes taking place in society and gain even a moiety of the new riches created by the machine. The reaction was triggered off by a member of the middle classes, George Birkbeck, a professor of Natural History, who launched a series of science lectures intended specifically for untutored manual workers. In Glasgow, in

The Great Exhibition in Hyde Park, 1851

1823, the informal series of classes became established as the first Mechanics' Institute, and over the next decade dozens were set up throughout the country. Their curricula rapidly abandoned the original limited but practical aims of introducing working men to the sciences that were immediately affecting their lives, and embarked instead on ambitious programmes of learning.

The Mechanics' Institute movement was not so much a dead end as a premature beginning. But its vigorous, spontaneous growth was characteristic of the society which gave it birth and which, at the very mid-century, produced that Great Exhibition which summed up the whole confident new age.

It was at a meeting of the Royal Society of Arts, held in Buckingham Palace, that Albert the Prince Consort arose and 'communicated his views regarding the formation of a Great

Sir Joseph Paxton, architect of the 'Crystal Palace'

Collection of Works of Industry and Art in London in 1851, for the purpose of exhibition and of competition and encouragement'. With his customary thoroughness, Albert went on to discuss the details of the Great Collection. Should it, for instance, be limited to British industry only? 'It was considered that, whilst it appears an error to fix any limitation to the production of machinery, science and taste, which are of no country but belong to the civilized world, particular advantage to British industry might be derived from placing it in fair competition with that of other nations.' The meeting had already come to the conclusion that the building, whatever form it might take, must be temporary, and Albert pointed out that the best site would be in Hyde Park. This was Crown Land, but as the meeting hastened to appoint His Royal Highness as head of the Royal Commission that would bring the Exhibition into being, little difficulty was anticipated in obtaining permission to use this land.

The decision to stage a Great Exhibition might have been born of simple emulation – France had had her Exposition in 1849. The Prince Consort might have supplied the dynamism as a means of employing his considerable talents in a non-controversial field. But the project immediately struck some spark in the British spirit and it was brought to fruition as a triumphant affirmation of national pride and confidence. The year 1851 marked the opening of a decade of prosperity from which most classes of society benefited. The idea of holding a holiday, of launching a project that was part fairground, part shop-window and wholly unprecedented, took firm hold on the public imagination. In an incredibly short space of time – a little over two years after that first, tentative meeting in Buckingham Palace – the immense structure opened its doors to the first of the four million people who would stream through them during the five months of the building's existence.

There were 27 men on the Royal Commission, but the Exhibition was essentially the work of three of them – the Prince Consort, the versatile public servant Henry Cole, and Joseph Paxton. Posterity has given most of the credit to Paxton, and it was fitting that the tumultuous period which was ushered in by the self-taught, self-made, gentle Thomas Telford, should be ushered out under the glass structure designed by the self-made, self-taught, ebullient Joseph Paxton. The son of a small farmer, he became head gardener to the Duke of Devonshire at Chatsworth, where he designed a glasshouse for a rare species of water-plant known as the *Victoria Regina*.

It was this glasshouse which provided the model for the

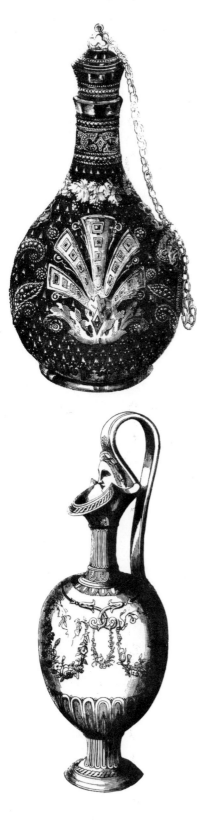

Great Exhibition building. The official design proposed was an enormous, solid, ugly brick structure, which aroused a storm of derision, and protests that the 'temporary' loan of Hyde Park was likely to prove only too permanent. Paxton then conceived the idea of designing a glass building which could be swiftly both erected and demolished. The Commission accepted his design, and work commenced in August 1850. Even as the building was intended to be a species of shrine to industry, so its erection could not have better demonstrated the new power of technology. Paxton boldly employed a form of pre-fabrication that was not used again for nearly a century. The organizing of the vast quantities of material – the thousands of tons of iron girders and trusses and posts, the thousands of feet of timber, the tons of putty, the hundreds of square yards of material and, above all, nearly a million square feet of glass – was of a very high order. Meanwhile the Prince presided over that section of the Commission which was deliberating on what was to be accepted for the Exhibition and who should be invited to send exhibits. Eventually, the whole civilized world was represented – every nation that had learned to tame steam, puddle iron, dig coal and shape the elements of the planet with machinery. The task of organizing the flow of exhibits was as complex as erecting the building itself. Over 100,000 objects arrived in Hyde Park, ranging from a case of stuffed cats in a ghastly eternal tea-party to pianofortes, stained glass, steam engines, parasols, threshing machines, printing presses and teasets – the inexhaustible cornucopia of an industrial civilization. The *Illustrated London News*, just recently embarked upon its long career, gratefully seized upon the occasion to fill page after page in issue after issue with descriptions of the artefacts, adopting a tone that was sometimes frivolous and sometimes impressed but always passionately interested. Its advertising columns, too, benefited, with offers as tempting as: 'A valuable, newly invented, very small, powerful waistcoat-pocket-glass, the size of a Walnut, to discern minute objects at a distance, which will be found to be very invaluable at the Exhibition.'

The Crystal Palace, as now all the world knew it, opened its doors at last on a bright, showery May morning in 1851.

Items to be seen at the Great Exhibition, from the Ceramics catalogue:
Top A delicate porcelain bottle
Left An Etruscan vase, by M. Copeland of London

Henry Mayhew turned aside from recording the dismal chronicles of the poor, the hungry and abandoned, and all those from whom the harnessed giant of industry had brought only despair and defeat, to record the apotheosis of the machine:

> As the morning advanced the crowds that came straggling on grew denser and denser, till at last it was one compact kind of road, paved with heads. On they went, fathers with their wives and children skipping jauntily along, and youths with their sweethearts in lovely coloured shawls and ribbons. All London and half the country and a good part of the world were wending their way to see the Queen pass in state to open the Great Exhibition of all the Nations.

And afterwards they passed, like pilgrims into a shrine, into the vast, gleaming Aladdin's cave of wealth whose heaped-up riches, produced by the machine, bore the promise that man need never again be hungry, or cold, or bored, or lonely.

Looking back at that immensely confident statement posterity can express only wonder and, perhaps, envy. A century after that brilliant flowering the worst social abuses created by the machine were laboriously being corrected. The numbers of those directly maimed or poisoned by it were steadily being reduced; the vile sprawl of buildings spawned to house the machine and its operatives was being cauterized. At the centenary of the Great Exhibition, the Festival of Britain in its turn could still proclaim that the machine, suitably controlled, was mankind's greatest ally. But as the flood of artefacts threaten to choke the civilization which created them, as the cities grow ever more monstrous and complex, above all, as the irreplaceable mineral fuels that powered the machines are transformed into inimical miasma, so there is emerging a truer indication of the price to be paid.

Opposite All the world on its way to the Great Exhibition, May 1851

THE
CRYSTAL PALACE QUADRILLE.

ENGLAND'S WELCOME TO THE NATIONS, with Portrait of Prince Albert (Song)	**6**d
QUADRILLE OF ALL NATIONS, with a View of the Palace	**6**d
THE PAXTON & CRYSTAL PALACE POLKAS	**3**d
THE GREAT EXHIBITION POLKA & GALOP	**3**d
THE GORLITZA OF ALL NATIONS	**3**d

The Great Exhibition in song

London:

G. H. DAVIDSON, 19, Peter's Hill St Paul's.

Suggestions for Further Reading

ALTICK, RICHARD, *Victorian People and Ideas*, London, 1974

ASHTON, T. S., *The Industrial Revolution, 1760–1830*, London 1964

BOVILL, E. W., *English Country Life*, London, 1962

BURNETT, JOHN, editor, *Useful Toil: autobiographies of working people from the 1820s to the 1920s*, London, 1974

CHADWICK, EDWIN, *Report on the Sanitary Condition of the Labouring Population of Great Britain* (edited by M. W. Flinn), Edinburgh, 1965

COBBETT, WILLIAM, *Rural Rides*, London, 1820

COBBETT, WILLIAM, *Cottage Economy*, London, 1823

COLEMAN, TERRY, *The Railway Navvies*, London, 1965

DERRY, T. K. and TREVOR I. WILLIAMS, *A Short History of Technology, from the earliest times to 1900*, London, 1960

DICKINSON, H. W., *A Short History of the Steam Engine*, Cambridge, 1939

EDEN, SIR FREDERIC MORTON, *The State of the Poor: a history of the labouring classes, with parochial reports*, London, 1928

ENGELS, FREDERICK, *The Condition of the Working Class in 1844*, London, 1920

FIELDING, HENRY, *A Proposal for Making an Effective Provision for the Poor*, London, 1753

FLINN, M. W., *The Origins of the Industrial Revolution*, London, 1966

GLASS, D. V., *Introduction to Malthus*, London, 1953

Great Exhibition 1851: *Official Description and Illustrated Catalogue*, London, 1851

HAMMOND, J. L. and B., *The Age of the Chartists*, London, 1930

HANWAY, JONAS, *A Sentimental History of Chimney Sweeps*, London, 1766

HARRISON, J. F. C., *The Early Victorians*, London, 1971

HOBHOUSE, CHRISTOPHER, *1851 and the Crystal Palace*

HOBSBAWM, E. J. and RUDÉ, GEORGE, *Captain Swing*, London, 1969

HOWITT, WILLIAM, *The Rural Life of England*, London, 1838

Illustrated London News Vol I, 1842 – Vol IX 1851

INGLIS, BRIAN, *Poverty and the Industrial Revolution*, London, 1971

MALTHUS, THOMAS, *An Essay on the Principle of Population*, London, 1798

MANTOUX, P., *The Industrial Revolution of the 18th Century*, London, 1928

MARSHALL, DOROTHY, *Industrial England, 1776–51*, London, 1973

MARTINEAU, HARRIETT, *Poor Laws and Paupers*, London, 1833–4

MAYHEW, HENRY, *London Labour and London Poor*, London, 1861–2

MITFORD, M. R., *Our Village*, London, 1839

OWEN, R., *Autobiography*, London, 1857

PARREAUX, ANDRÉ, *Daily Life in England in the Reign of George III* (translated by Carola Congreve), London, 1961

PUCKLER-MUSKAU, PRINCE, *A Regency Visitor* (ed E. M. Butler), London, 1957

PUDNEY, JOHN, *Brunel and his World*, London, 1974

RUSH, RICHARD, *The Court of London from 1819 to 1825*, London, 1873

STIRLING, A. M. W., *Coke of Norfolk and his Friends*, London, 1908

SURTEES, R. S., *Jorrocks' Jaunts and Jollities*, London

SURTEES, R. S., *Town and Country Papers* (ed E. D. Cummings), London, 1929

TAYLER, WILLIAM, *Autobiography* (*see* Burnett)

THOMPSON, E. P., *The Making of the English Working Class*, London, 1963

TREASE, GEOFFREY, *Nottingham: a biography*, London

Index